The former publisher and executive vice president of *Facts On File*, **Edward W. Knappman** has acquired and edited more than 400 reference books during his publishing career. His previously published books include *Great American Trials* and *American Jobs Abroad*, both from Visible Ink Press.

A criminal defense attorney with more than 25 years experience, **Roy Black** practices law in Miami and successfully defended William Kennedy Smith in Palm Beach, Florida, in 1991. The noted trial was given gavel-to-gavel coverage by television networks and was viewed by millions of Americans.

SEX,
SIN
&
MAYHEM

SEX, SIN & MAYHEM

NOTORIOUS TRIALS OF THE '90S

edited by Edward W. Knappman

A New England Publishing Associates book

Detroit • New York • Toronto • Washington, D.C.

Sex, Sin & Mayhem

Published by **Visible Ink Press**™
a division of Gale Research Inc.

Visible Ink Press is a trademark of Gale Research Inc.

Art Director: Mary Krzewinski

Typesetting by the Graphix Group

Library of Congress Cataloging-in-Publication Data

Sex, sin & mayhem : notorious trials of the '90s / edited by Edward W. Knappman

      p.   cm.
   Includes index.
   ISBN 0-7876-0476-3 (acid-free paper)
   1. Trials—United States.   I. Knappman, Edward W.
KF220.S49   1995
347.73'7—dc20
[347.3077]   95-21959
                                        CIP

10 9 8 7 6 5 4 3 2

Printed in the United States of America

CONTENTS

FOREWORD

THE POWER OF TV
by Criminal Defense Attorney Roy Black

On a sweltering hot Florida morning, I walked down Dixie Highway, past parking lots jammed with satellite trucks, and I paused to watch workmen build wooden scaffolding for temporary news anchor desks. I marveled at the mountains of exotic electronic gear and the miles of multi-colored cables connecting it all. I had an appointment in court, so as quickly as the heat would allow, I walked the next block and turned into the Palm Beach County Courthouse Plaza. Suddenly, I was assaulted by a phalanx of cameramen led by brazen reporters thrusting boom microphones and rude questions in my face. Momentarily stunned, I quickly shouldered my way through the mob and into Courtroom 411. Just inside the courtroom doors was a huge studio-sized television camera sporting its own mounted operator, and as I walked around it, I saw a row of photographers armed with an arsenal of telephoto lenses. The camera and the lenses followed me all the way to the counsel table.

It was the first day of jury selection for the *William Kennedy Smith* trial, and the nation—even the world—would hang on my every word in the courtroom. My experience is no longer unique. This is the '90s, and the courts have entered into an uneasy partnership with television.

I futilely tried to hold back the future by filing motion after motion to exclude the camera. I ticked off the traditional

> **I** was personally afraid of this radical change. . . . I felt real fear knowing a national TV audience . . . would be watching my every action, hearing my every word, and second-guessing all of them.

legal complaints against television: it distorted and demeaned justice, frightened witnesses, intimidated jurors, and turned lawyers into flamboyant actors in a soap opera (not me, of course). But to be brutally honest, these solid legal arguments were not the only reason I fought so hard against the camera; I was personally afraid of this radical change in criminal trials. I felt real fear knowing a national TV audience, encouraged by astute legal commentators, would be watching my every action, hearing my every word, and second-guessing all of them. I soon discovered the power of those TV camera lenses.

One afternoon, the camera panned over my shoulder, focused on my legal pad, and a national audience was treated to a display of my best doodles. In the end, Judge Mary Lupo chuckled and denied all my motions, proving she was far wiser than I.

Television has proven it deserves a permanent place in our courtrooms. It is the public's window on—their front row seat for—the dramatic trials of our time. We should not be surprised at the popularity of the celebrity criminal trials because they capture our attention as few public events can. The nail-biting suspense of a true story unfolding in a tense courtroom is far more addictive than any Hollywood film story. Each of the trials played out in these pages aroused powerful emotions. They caused us to think about and then debate such social issues as child abuse, racism, male-female relationships, and insanity. The interest in these issues was so intense that several verdicts caused a reshaping of public policy. If a televised trial is a catalyst for public discussion of legal and social issues, why should we unplug it?

If a televised trial is a catalyst for public discussion of legal and social issues, why should we unplug it?

My personal view, after spending twenty-five years in courtrooms throughout this country, is that the public scrutiny through the use of television keeps the system honest and accountable. It is the best deterrent to abusive judges, overzealous prosecutors, and negligent or indifferent defense lawyers. How long could a politically motivated witch hunt survive the unblinking scrutiny of Court TV?

But we still have not gone far enough. While thirty-four states allow cameras in criminal court, last year the Federal Judicial Conference pulled the plug on a three-year pilot program that allowed the televising of selected federal civil trials. This was a tragic step backward for our democracy. The proof is easy to come by. I can only imagine the public's reaction if they had watched a tough little hoodlum named Sammy "The Bull" Gravano confess to nineteen murders on the witness stand, yet be sentenced to only five years in prison because he gave testimony against well-known Mafia boss John Gotti. The camera exposes—not causes—flaws in our system.

The shortcomings of cameras in the courtroom are far outweighed by the benefit of allowing every citizen, with his or her own eyes, to watch justice in action. For the first time in our history, the Sixth Amendment prescription of a public trial is truly fulfilled.

INTRODUCTION

Ancient Rome had its circuses, and late-twentieth-century America has its criminal trials. However momentous trials may be for the participants—indeed they may be literally matters of life and death, for most of us they are primarily public spectacles, with the competing gladiators dressed in three-piece suits.

Never has this been more apparent than in the 1990s. The advent of Court TV and tabloid television shows has made "trial junkies" out of tens of millions of Americans. Late night talk show hosts make lawyers, defendants, witnesses, and even judges the butt of one liners and spoof their mannerisms, supremely confident that the audience will get the jokes. In an innovation of the 1990s, the major networks have begun hiring famous criminal attorneys to provide play-by-play "color commentary" in a broadcast format previously associated with the coverage of professional sports. The O.J. Simpson trial so dominated the television news that one critic quipped that Cable News Network (CNN) should adopt a new slogan: The All O.J., All the Time Network.

The boundaries in American popular culture between news and entertainment, fact and fiction, have always been a bit blurred, but the 1990s have seen such lines of demarcation virtually erased. Made-for-TV movies repackage and "re-enact" dozens of major trials for viewers whose appetites aren't satiated by the real trials or who prefer a more polished dramatic structure than the messy legal process affords. Tabloid television reporters race prosecutors and defense attorneys to secure the testimony of potential witnesses, but sometimes have the advantage of offering wads of cash for "exclusive stories" that can be aired even before the jury hears them.

Of course, trials have always been a popular form of entertainment and public ritual in American life. Since the country's founding, in person and through the news media, Americans have flocked to courtrooms to be titillated, scandalized, uplifted, inspired, educated, and just plain amused. Before the age of mass communications, the local courthouse provided one of the few diversions available to a largely rural population. Indeed, judges, preachers, and editorial writers have so long and frequently denounced the "circus-like" atmosphere prevailing at many locally or nationally celebrated trials that the phrase has become a cliché of courtroom journalism.

While the news media's and the public's obsession with sensational trials may prompt clucking from moralists, what matters most about the American court system, ultimately, is its public nature. Open trials and public scrutiny are fundamental to our respect for law and essential for the psychological well-being of society. Not only does public attention protect us all from an arbitrary judicial system, public trials fulfill a basic human need for retribution and provide even the losers with a sense that he or she at least has had an opportunity to present a case, or as the cliché states, to have his or her day in court.

> **J**udges, preachers, and editorial writers have so long and frequently denounced the "circus-like" atmosphere . . . that the phrase has become a cliché of courtroom journalism.

I have selected the trials described in *Sex, Sin & Mayhem* primarily on the basis of the interest they generated. Undeniably, the book was written and edited more to entertain than to educate readers. However, we have made every effort to be scrupulously factual and to avoid sensationalizing events that were already quite sensational. If there is any conclusion to be drawn from the 26 recent trials recounted in *Sex, Sin & Mayhem*, it is that all sensational trials have one common element: they explore motives of lust, greed and fear—the primordial human emotions.

Many people made vital contributions to the writing, editing and production of *Sex, Sin & Mayhem*. At Visible Ink Press, Marty Connors conceived this book; Rebecca Nelson calmly and confidently ushered it through an extraordinarily tight production schedule. For meeting our rigorous deadlines and saving us potential bloopers, I owe thanks to Roberta Buland for her copy-editing, to Winifred Bonney for her proofreading and indexing, and especially to Vicki Harlow for her resourceful picture research. Julia Daniel kept an eye on the headlines and researched some of the more obscure facts.

The greatest credit for this book, however, must be reserved for the writers: Colin Evans, Penelope Petzhold, Bernie Ryan, and Tom Smith.

Edward W. Knappman

After six years as Colonel Robert Hogan in the popular television comedy, *Hogan's Heroes* and one season starring in his own sitcom, which was not a success, actor Bob Crane hit America's dinner theater circuit. A tour stop at the Windmill Dinner Theater took the 49-year-old Crane to the Phoenix suburb of Scottsdale, Arizona, where he settled into a rented apartment for the duration of the run of *Beginner's Luck.* Crane's performance in the play did not attract headlines, but he did make the front page on June 29, 1978. That afternoon, at about 2 P.M., he had been found murdered in his bed. His skull had been smashed with a blunt object while he slept. An electrical cord was tied loosely around his neck.

Nothing of obvious value had been stolen from the apartment. Police could find no murder weapon or witnesses, but they immediately suspected Crane's friend and traveling companion, John Henry Carpenter. A national electronics executive with plenty of experience operating video camera equipment, Carpenter was a perfect pal for Crane, whose two favorite hobbies were photography and sex. The pair enjoyed cruising bars where Crane's celebrity attracted women. The actor frequently brought starstruck admirers back to his room. With and sometimes without their permission, he would videotape sex acts with his female guests and take Polaroid snapshots of them. Carpenter was often invited to share in his friend's luck with women, sometimes on camera.

Police found a video camera in the dead man's living room. They also discovered photographic developing equipment in his bathroom along with explicit examples of his celluloid conquests. Investigators learned that Crane's personal photo album of sexual escapades was missing from the apartment. It was possible that a cuckolded spouse or jealous boyfriend might figure in the killing.

Yet, the focus seemed fixed on Crane's relationship with Carpenter, who had been in Scottsdale. The two men had been seen having a tense conversation in a restaurant earlier that week. Although Carpenter's flight back to California the day of the killing was planned far in advance, it was his awkward phone calls to Crane's family before news of the murder became public that aroused police suspicions. Crane's eldest son, Robert Crane, Jr., recalled that his father had been lately annoyed with Carpenter's constant presence and had been thinking of ending their friendship. When Carpenter called the Crane household, he ended the conversation with Bobby by telling Crane's son that if he needed anything to please contact him. Scottsdale detectives interviewed Carpenter several times. They were sure they had enough evidence to arrest him.

In 1949, Crane married Ann Terzian, his high school sweetheart. The couple had three children—Robert, Jr., Deborah, and Karen. But in 1968, Ann discovered her husband was having an affair with *Hogan's Heroes* actress Sigrid Valdis (real name Patricia Olsen). A few weeks after the Cranes divorced in 1970, Crane wed Valdis on the set of the TV program. She was pregnant at the time.

However, the case looked like a forensic scientist's worst nightmare to Maricopa County Attorney Charles Hyder. Undertrained Scottsdale police had mishandled the investigation from the beginning. The crime scene had not been secured; cops had wandered in and out of the apartment at will. No one questioned moving men working at the apartment complex that day. Victoria Berry, the actress who had discovered Crane's body, remained in the apartment answering the telephone during the investigation.

There was confusion over whether or not police had collected everything they found in a single garbage bag; potential evidence should have been isolated. Although Carpenter was a prime suspect, his hotel room was never searched. Making matters worse,

Crane's son, Bobby, and business manager, Lloyd Vaughan, were allowed to remove some of Crane's possessions from his apartment the day after the killing. Perhaps most crucial of all, human tissue found at the scene was destroyed without ever having been tested.

Maricopa County Attorney Hyder felt that the sloppy handling of the case would make a successful prosecution impossible. Angry Scottsdale detectives remained convinced that Carpenter had killed Crane, but they could not convince Hyder or his successor to bring the case to court. No charges were filed. Controversy over the unsolved murder made it a perennial campaign issue in Maricopa County politics.

Investigators looked into Crane's prolific sexual activities and found no fresh leads. Meanwhile, John Carpenter's personal life became a nightmare. Nationally identified as the main suspect in the Bob Crane murder, he remained in California with the stigma of the unsolved crime clinging to him.

Fourteen years later, on June 1, 1992, County Attorney Rick Romley announced that new evidence would enable him to indict a suspect. In Carson, California, Carpenter was arrested on his way to work, extradited to Arizona, and charged with first-degree murder. He was released on $98,000 bail, but the arrest took its toll. He lost his job and his house. The court appointed a public defender to represent him.

When his case reached court in September 1994, the prosecution unfurled the scenario that had convinced detectives for so long that Carpenter was their man. Authorities who had previously declined to provide any motive for the brutal murder now revealed their theory that the common obsession for sex, which had bound Crane and Carpenter together, was ultimately responsible for the actor's death.

Carpenter "fed off the energy and fame of the actor," prosecutor Robert Shutts told the jury in his opening statement. "Bob Crane became a source of women that he could never obtain for himself."

The prosecution charged that when it became clear to Carpenter that Crane would end their friendship and by so doing end Carpenter's plentiful supply of attractive sex partners, Carpenter crushed the actor's skull with a video camera tripod while the actor slept.

To illustrate Crane's and Carpenter's habits as "swingers," jurors were shown a strategically altered black-and-white home-

made video of both men simultaneously having sex with a woman. Another woman, who shared Crane's bed the night before the murder, testified that the actor told her he was tired of Carpenter's constant presence.

Prosecutors presented their single piece of new evidence—a police photograph, which upon close inspection showed a small speck on the passenger-side door panel of Carpenter's rented white 1978 Chrysler Cordoba. To forensic investigators, the 1/16th of an inch speck looked like a globule of fatty brain tissue. A medical examiner testified that the matter in the photograph might be human tissue, but admitted he could not be certain. Public defenders Stephen Avilla and Candace Hewitt Kent called their own medical expert, who doubted that the speck was of human origin. Explaining that subcutaneous fat tissue would have excreted grease in the Arizona heat, the defense expert noted that no grease smears surrounded the speck. Laboratory tests of the matter might have provided a definitive analysis, but Scottsdale investigators had lost the sample.

"They don't have anything," said Defense Attorney Avilla, brushing aside the prosecution's motive theory as nothing more than lurid speculation. Outside of court, the defense charged that the County Attorney's political ambitions were driving a prosecution that would be doomed by the carelessness of the original investigation. Avilla also told the press that one of the moving men working outside Crane's apartment building on the morning of the murder had come forward. The witness reported having seen a man exit Crane's apartment and leave in a white Cadillac, not a Cordoba. The driver, said the moving man, did not resemble Carpenter.

Inside the courtroom, attorneys Avilla and Kent aggressively attacked the bungled investigation that had kept the case out of court for years. Alleged brain tissue was not the only evidence missing from the case: The murder weapon—described as a "blunt linear instrument"—was never found and though the prosecutors argued that a missing video camera tripod was the deadly object, the defense's medical expert said that only a heavier object like a tire iron or crowbar could have crushed Crane's temple.

A small stain on the vinyl interior door panel of Carpenter's car had been analyzed after the killing and was said to have

John H. Carpenter discusses his case with Attorney Gary Fleischman during a June 1, 1992, courtroom appearance. Carpenter was charged with the murder of television star, Bob Crane, of the well-known *Hogan's Heroes* show. Bob Crane, 49, was found murdered in a motel with his skull crushed and an electric cord tied around his neck.

matched Crane's blood type. But it also matched the blood type of over a quarter of a million people in the greater Phoenix area. "DNA fingerprint" testing had been invented in the years since the murder, but no genetic comparison with the victim was possible since the original test evidence was missing, and a 1990 test of the door panel came up negative for the presence of blood. If tiny bits of Bob Crane had been on the inside of John Carpenter's rented Cordoba, authorities were now unable to prove it.

Werner Klemperer, *Hogan's Heroes* commanding officer Colonel Klink, remembers Crane as "a very gregarious, outgoing person with a great sense of humor." Crane's youngest son, Scott, now a recording-studio owner in Seattle, describes his father as a loving and playful man.

—*People,* September 1994

During the trial, Carpenter was not called to testify in his own defense. On October 31, 1994, after two and a half days of jury deliberations, he was found not guilty. The 66-year-old defendant and his wife burst into tears.

The jurors had been unimpressed by the mystery speck in the photograph. "If you don't have evidence," the jury foreman said, "you can't find someone guilty on speculation."

"My life is back together again after 16 years," Carpenter told reporters. "I feel like a 10,000 pound weight has been lifted off my head."

As in most trials, relief over an acquittal was not felt by everyone. Public Defender Avilla riled County Attorney Romley by accusing prosecutors of wasting more than a million dollars in public funds on a flimsy case.

Crane's children and friends, some of whom had long wondered aloud why so few suspects had been investigated, were left with a painful memory that showed little hope of being put to rest.

—Tom Smith

For years Washington, D.C., buzzed with rumors that Mayor Marion Barry had a drug problem. Concrete proof came on January 18, 1990, when Barry entered Room 726 at the Vista International Hotel to keep an assignation with ex-girlfriend, Rasheeda Moore. After rejecting Barry's sexual advance, Moore produced a pipe for smoking cocaine (Barry had earlier given Moore $20 to buy some crack cocaine). Seconds after Barry put the pipe to his lips, half a dozen FBI agents and other police officers rushed into the room and arrested him. The sting had worked perfectly: Every incident had been captured on videotape.

On June 19, 1990, Prosecutor Richard Roberts outlined Barry's six-year involvement with drugs, emphasizing the mayor's hypocrisy: "During the course of this trial, you will learn that while the defendant preached 'Down with dope!' he was putting dope up his nose . . . every person has two sides . . . this case is about the other side, the secret side of Marion Barry."

The star prosecution witness was Charles Lewis, a confessed drug dealer. He first met Barry in the Virgin Islands in June 1986. "He asked me if I could get some rocks [crack cocaine] . . . I told him, 'yes.'" According to Lewis, Barry's drug binge included straight cocaine and marijuana as well.

Chief Defense Counsel Kenneth Mundy, deriding Lewis's

claim that conscience had prompted his testimony, scoffed, "You didn't wake up and start cooperating [with the authorities] until you got convicted in the Virgin Islands, is that correct?"

"Both things happened at the same time."

"You were facing big time, weren't you?"

"The reason I waited. . . . "

"Is that a yes or a no?" barked Mundy.

"Yes," Lewis admitted.

For three days Mundy kept up the attack, extracting one damaging concession after another from an increasingly pathetic Lewis. It was a superb feat of advocacy, one that gave the prosecution pause for thought: Perhaps their case wasn't so airtight after all.

Help for the prosecution was at hand in Rasheeda Moore. She detailed a three-year liaison with Barry, plagued with drugs and occasional violence, putting the prosecution back on track. It was during her testimony that the Vista videotape was played. Mundy grilled Moore about her background, hardly exemplary, portraying her as out to get Barry because he had ditched her for another woman. He also scored points with her admission that she had used drugs in April 1990, three months after the Vista sting.

See it on the big screen: Before he was re-elected mayor, *Time* reported that Barry visited Hollywood producer Ron Samuels, who said that if Barry were re-elected, a movie about his life would be "even more of a Rocky story."

"It's something I have to deal with every day," said Moore, referring to her cocaine addiction. When Mundy suggested that the receipt of several thousand dollars from the government had loosened her tongue, Moore demurred. She said her decision to set Barry up had resulted from a revival of religious belief.

Because Barry declined to testify on his own behalf, the defense was comprised mainly of witnesses who placed Barry elsewhere at times when he was supposed to have participated in alleged drug deals.

On August 2, 1990, the jury began deliberations. More than a week later it announced that it was hopelessly deadlocked on all except two counts, one guilty, the other not guilty. Judge Thomas Jackson had no alternative but to declare a mistrial on the remaining 12 charges. Later, in a rare public attack, Judge Jackson suggested that some jurors had been less than forthcoming about their true feelings during the impanelment process. He told a Harvard Law School class that he had "never seen a stronger government case" than the one mounted against Barry.

The final act in this drama came on October 26, 1990, when Judge Jackson sentenced Barry to six months in prison, a fine and probation. The verdict derailed Barry's political career, reinforcing the perception in some quarters that that had been the intent all along. But after completing his jail term, Barry was elected in November 1992 to Washington's city council.

The most remarkable political comeback in recent U.S. history continued. Apparently perceived by the Washington electorate as more sinned against than sinning, Barry stunned his detractors on September 14, 1994, by winning the Democratic nomination for Mayor of the city, the very position he had disgraced just four years earlier. In the primary, he emphatically trounced both of his rivals, including incumbent Mayor Sharon Pratt Kelly who received just

With his wife at his side, Marion Barry prepares to give his acceptance speech after being sworn in for a fourth term as the mayor of Washington, D.C., in November 1994. Barry's political career was temporarily halted in the summer of 1990 when he was charged with drug offenses and found guilty on one count of cocaine possession. AP/Wide World Photos

"He quintessentially represents hope, more so than anybody running in the race and maybe anybody who can run." —Rock Newman, Barry friend and head of his transition team, quoted in a December 5, 1994, *Chicago Tribune* story headlined "Second Chance / The Young, Down-trodden Give Barry Another Lease as Mayor of Washington"

13 percent of the vote. At the November 8 election, Barry's margin of victory was no less impressive as he garnered 54 percent of the vote to doom the mayoral ambitions of Carol Schwartz, a white Republican: Washington, D.C., is an over-whelmingly African-American city where registered Democrats outnumber Republicans by more than four to one.

With a budget deficit of half a billion dollars and the third highest murder rate in America, Washington, D.C., is clearly in a desperate plight. However, when Barry was once again sworn in as mayor on January 2, 1995, he sounded hopeful: "God helped me get out of the valley, and I'm going to use the same prayers, the same vision to help the city overcome." He also promised to resign if his drug problems ever resurfaced.

—Colin Evans

lisabeth Anne Broderick was ill-prepared and emotionally devastated when her 16-year marriage to Attorney Daniel Broderick III shattered in 1985. The end of the marriage cost two people their lives and provoked discussion about the way American courts treat women in divorce settlements.

For Dan Broderick, wealthy president of the San Diego County Bar Association, the nightmare began when he had an affair with an attractive, young legal assistant, Linda Kolkena. Although Dan had left home, his wife Betty refused to let go of him emotionally. She burned the clothes he left behind and later, when she was visiting her children at Dan's new home, she smeared his new wardrobe with a pie. He requested a restraining order. In retaliation, she threw a wine bottle through his window. When he ordered her off his property, she drove her van into the door he had slammed in her face. She refused to accept a financial settlement so that he could get on with his life.

When Betty left a nasty message on Dan's telephone answering machine, he used the tape to convince a judge to issue a contempt citation. Months of obscene messages and contempt hearings followed, including one that earned Betty six days in jail.

In Betty Broderick's nightmare, the petty vandalism and verbal outbursts were natural. Deserting her for a younger woman was only the first of her husband's many betrayals. When Betty left their four

Deputy District Attorney Kerry Wells cross-examines accused murderer, Betty Broderick, during her second trial in November 1991. Courtesy Office of Deputy District Attorney, San Diego

children at his new home unannounced, trying to make a point that raising them was not her responsibility alone, he kept the children.

Under California's no-fault divorce law, the Brodericks' marriage was dissolved quickly. Dividing their property and determining custody of their children, however, dragged on in court for years. Dan argued that his successful law practice had been the result of his own work. Representing herself, Betty responded that she had constantly supported Dan, particularly in their early years together. She charged him with underestimating the worth of his practice to cheat her out of a fair division settlement.

The court's decision was almost entirely favorable to the husband. Exactly as he had requested, Dan got custody of their two young sons, and Betty got custody of their rebellious 17-year-old daughter. The elder Broderick daughter was by then living on her own. The judge also accepted Dan's self-appraised financial statements. While Betty was awarded $16,000 in monthly support, it amounted to a tiny fraction of her husband's monetary worth. Eleven weeks after the divorce decree was announced in January 1989, Linda Kolkena and Dan Broderick were married. Betty hired attorneys to appeal the financial and custodial edicts.

Unrelieved rage was one of the few things Betty had not lost. Before the appeals process could get started, Betty shot Dan and Linda Broderick to death in their bed, ripped the phone out of the wall and drove away. The shootings occurred on November 5, 1989. Betty surrendered to police later that day.

Judge Thomas Whelan tried to keep Betty Broderick's trial focused on the two deaths. When the trial began in 1990, he ruled that the financial terms of the Broderick divorce were not to be discussed. No testimony critical of the character of Dan and Linda Broderick would be permitted unless it related to Betty Broderick's state of mind on the night of the killings.

Broderick's sympathizers may have seen her as a victim, but Deputy District Attorney Kerry Wells saw the defendant as a murderer, not a martyr.

"I've had my fill of Elisabeth Broderick," Wells would say scornfully. "She was not a battered woman. She was given $16,000 a month in alimony. She had a million-dollar La Jolla house, a car, a boyfriend. I see abused women every day with broken bones and smashed faces. Give me a break!"

Wells portrayed Broderick as a selfish woman whose obsessive refusal to concede that her marriage was over resulted from narcissism and financial greed. The divorce had reduced Betty's income and social status. Her reaction, argued the prosecution, was a consuming jealous hatred that led her to kill.

Psychoanalysts disagreed over whether Broderick was an emotionally battered woman or a self-absorbed schemer. The answering machine tapes Dan Broderick had used as legal ammunition were played. Although Betty was on trial for murder, not vulgarity, the blue language on the tapes gave the prosecution a weapon it used repeatedly.

Defense Attorney Jack Earley tried to impress the jury with the cause of his client's decline. Even though accusations of adultery were inadmissable, testimony critical of Dan and Linda Broderick crept into the case. Betty spoke of Dan's drinking and suspicions that Linda had anonymously sent her hate mail. There was also Linda's paralegal needling: She had signed official and emotionally charged documents addressed to Betty, including a letter informing the former Mrs. Broderick of her removal from Dan's family medical insurance policy.

When Oprah Winfrey interviewed Broderick from prison in March 1992, the talk show scored its second-highest ratings to date. —*Ladies' Home Journal*, December 1992

Betty testified that she had gone to Dan and Linda Broderick's bedroom to beg Dan to stop his legal assault on her child custody rights. If he would not listen, she said she would kill herself. She claimed to remember little of what happened next.

While prosecutor Wells aired countless ugly confrontations between the Brodericks, she never examined the defendant about what happened on the night of the killings. This was a serious omission. After four days of deliberations, jurors announced that they were deadlocked. Judge Whelan declared a mistrial.

From prison, Betty gave frequent interviews about the bad hand she felt her husband and the courts had dealt her. The case attracted the sympathy of many women who identified with the betrayals she had suffered. Others thought she was a paragon of self pity.

When Betty returned to San Diego Superior Court for her retrial in September 1991, the defense attempted to illustrate that the shootings had resulted from panic, not deliberate aim. This time prosecutor Wells pressed Betty to describe what happened in the bedroom.

Linda had screamed, "Call the police!" Dan had grabbed the phone, Betty recalled. She fired reflexively into the darkness and fled. She recalled little else.

Broderick's testimony became increasingly argumentative and rambling as her failed marriage was dissected once again. Then her attorney dropped a bombshell. He asked if her husband had ever planned to have her killed. Shocked, she answered, "no." Attorney Earley then divulged the name of a man to whom Dan Broderick had allegedly spoken about having his wife killed.

Furious prosecutors succeeded in disallowing Earley's remarks, but reporters located three people, including a deputy district attorney, with whom Dan Broderick had discussed killing his wife. A fourth witness volunteered to testify that Linda Broderick had told him that she and Dan were trying to hasten Betty's mental collapse with relentless legal moves.

Yet, the jury never heard these allegations. Judge Whelan ruled that since Betty was unaware of any threats, they had not influenced her actions, and were thus inadmissable. The judge then forbade the attorneys to discuss the case with the press.

Betty's obscene phone messages were replayed. Even more jarring were conversations in which the Broderick's sobbing young sons pleaded with their mother to stop her vulgar verbal attacks so that they could spend time with her. Dan Broderick's choosing to secretly tape the calls rather than terminate them in order to spare his children this emotional abuse spoke volumes about his subtle manipulations. Yet it was Betty's foul-mouthed browbeating and hatred that rang in the courtroom.

The state wanted Broderick convicted on two counts of premeditated first-degree murder. Her attorney argued that the emotional battering she had suffered at her husband's hands had shat-

Crime scene and home of the murder victims, Daniel and Linda Kolkena Broderick. Courtesy Office of Deputy District Attorney, San Diego

tered her ability to plan anything, let alone a double murder. Earley asked the jury to find her guilty of manslaughter.

The jury chose to convict Betty Broderick on two counts of second-degree murder. It decided that she had not planned the murders, but had acted with malicious intent. Judge Whelan sentenced her to two consecutive fifteen-years-to-life terms.

Publicity over the Broderick divorce sparked activism in California to make custody and financial settlements fairer to women in that state. Yet nothing seemed to provide any emotional closure for Broderick. She continued to rail against her dead ex-husband until television reporters finally stopped coming, leaving her to wait for her first eligible parole date in the year 2011.

—Tom Smith

According to *People* magazine, prison officials at the Central California Women's Facility in Chowchilla, report that Broderick gets along so well with the other inmates that she is known as the "cruise director" in the yard.

PAMELA SMART TRIAL

On May 1, 1990, just one week before his first wedding anniversary, Gregory Smart, a 24-year-old insurance salesman, was shot dead at his Derry, New Hampshire, condominium during what appeared to be a botched burglary. Six weeks later William Flynn, 16, Vance Lattime, 17, and Patrick Randall, 18, all Winnacunnet High School students, were arrested and charged with the murder. All three pleaded guilty. In return for reduced sentences, the teenagers agreed to testify against the person they claimed had persuaded them to carry out the killing— Pamela Smart, the wife of the dead man.

When oral arguments commenced on March 4, 1991, Assistant Attorney General Diane Nicolosi portrayed the teenagers as naive victims of an evil woman bent on murder. Nicolosi claimed that Smart, a 22-year-old Winnacunnet High School teacher, seduced Flynn with the sole intent of duping him into murdering her husband, so that she might avoid an expensive divorce and benefit from a $140,000 life insurance policy.

Graphic details of the murder were provided by Patrick Randall. He told how Flynn had enlisted his services, together with Vance Lattime, and how all three had gone to the Smart residence. While Lattime waited outside, Flynn and Randall ransacked the condominium, then ambushed Greg Smart when he returned home from a sales meeting. Randall admitted to holding a knife at Smart's throat as Flynn fired a .38 caliber bullet through the vic-

Police investigators enter the New Hampshire condominium complex of Gregory Smart after he was murdered by three high school students at the instigation of his wife, a high school teacher. Geoff Forester/*Concord Monitor*

tim's brain. Afterward, the two took some jewelry to create the impression of a robbery gone wrong.

Defense counsel Mark Sisti bitterly denounced all Randall's allegations, noting that only in the course of plea bargaining had he implicated Pamela Smart.

"Pamela Smart didn't make you kill anybody, right?" Sisti asked.

"No," agreed Randall.

"You went to kill Greg Smart for your friend Bill [Flynn], right?"

"Yes."

"Pamela Smart had nothing to do with that, correct?"

"Correct," Randall admitted.

Vance Lattime, driver of the getaway car, told the jury that Smart gave him a pair of stereo speakers and promised an additional $250 for his part in the slaying. He added that, prior to the murder, she had asked the other gang members how she should act upon finding her husband's body. "She didn't know whether to scream, run from house to house or call the police. We told her just to act normal." About one point Lattime was adamant—that Smart had insisted they shoot rather than stab her husband because she didn't want blood spattered over her white furniture. There was also testimony that Smart had instructed Flynn not to shoot her husband in front of their dog so the animal wouldn't be traumatized.

When William Flynn took the stand, he tearfully recounted how Smart had seduced him, interspersing the sexual blandishments with repeated and more urgent stories of the physical abuse Greg had inflicted on his wife, especially one incident when he had locked her out of the house in the winter while she was clad only in her nightclothes. Flynn said, "She started crying and said the only way she could see for us to be together was if we killed Greg." At first, Flynn doubted Smart's seriousness, but as her temper and threats worsened, he yielded to her demands. "I was afraid if I didn't do it, she would leave me."

To an emotion-packed courtroom, Flynn described how he had put the revolver to Smart's head, then uttered "God, forgive me," before pulling the trigger.

"Why did you say 'God, forgive me'?" asked Assistant Attorney General Paul Maggiotto.

"Because I didn't want to kill Greg," said Flynn. "I wanted to be with Pam, and that's what I had to do to be with Pam."

During her college radio days at Florida State University, Smart called herself the Maiden of Metal. Smart remained a fan of heavy metal music even after graduating in 1988.

Of all the prosecution witnesses, none created more impact or did more damage than Cecelia Pierce, 16, another Winnacunnet High School student. She repeated a conversation with Smart: "I have a choice: either kill Greg or get a divorce," she quoted Smart as saying. "I told her to get a divorce." Asked how Smart had responded, Pierce replied, "She said she couldn't, because Greg would take the dog and the furniture and she wouldn't have any money or a place to live."

Pierce did admit prior knowledge of the murder plot, even to the point of aiding Smart in her search for a gun, but Pierce claimed that afterward conscience led her to the police. At their behest, she

Questioned by prosecutor Paul Maggiotto, Pamela Smart testifies in her own defense on March 18, 1991, at the Rockingham Superior Court in Exeter, New Hampshire. Courtesy of *Foster's Daily Democrat*, Dover, NH

secretly taped several conversations with Smart. In one, Smart ordered Pierce to keep quiet; otherwise they would all "go to the slammer for the rest of our entire lives." On another occasion, Smart boasted of committing the perfect murder.

Sisti cast a pall over much of this testimony by revealing that Pierce had already sold the rights to her story to a Hollywood production company for a considerable sum of money. "What this all comes down to," he said, "is that you have a shot at $100,000 . . . and you claim to have been Pam's best friend?"

"Yes," admitted Pierce.

Throughout the proceedings Pamela Smart had maintained an icy composure, but contrition took over in the witness box. She claimed that her attempts to break off the affair with Flynn had been thwarted by his threats of suicide. "I was devastated," she said. While conceding the impropriety of their relationship, Smart vehemently denied any suggestion that she had planned murder. "I didn't force anybody to kill Greg!"

Then why, wondered Maggiotto, had she made those statements to Cecelia Pierce? That had been a subterfuge, Smart said, all part of her own investigation into the murder of her husband.

"What were you going to do?" asked Maggiotto, "Make a citizen's arrest?"

"No."

"Or was Pam Smart going to use her own investigation skills . . . and write a report and mail it in?"

"Yes," replied Smart, blaming her apparent instability on some heavy medication she was taking at the time she was going to make the report.

It was Smart's position, as it had been for the defense from the outset, that the murder was solely the work of the three teenagers, who now saw a way to ameliorate their sentences by implicating her. "They murdered Greg," she cried. "They're the ones who broke into the house. They waited for him. And they're the ones who brought him to his knees and brought a knife to his throat before shooting him!"

Derry police reported that Flynn had bungled an earlier attempt on Greg Smart's life when he had become lost on his way to the Smarts's condominium.

The jury took 13 hours to decide Smart's fate. She stood emotionless as the guilty verdict was read. When Judge Douglas Gray imposed a life sentence without the possibility of parole, she seemed equally unaffected.

For their involvement in the murder, both Flynn and Randall were sentenced to 28 years to life. Vance Lattime received 18 years to life. Yet another student who knew of the plot, Raymond Fowler, also pleaded guilty to conspiracy and was jailed for 15 to 30 years.

In a made-for-TV movie, *Murder In New Hampshire,* Pamela Smart was depicted as a scheming architect of murder. While the pertinency of that view is a matter of record, often overlooked is the ease with which her young lover was able to recruit assistants for his deadly mission. In this extraordinary case there was more than enough blame for everyone.

On March 11, 1993, it was announced that Smart had been moved from the New Hampshire State Prison for Women in Goffstown, New Hampshire, to Bedford Hills Correctional Facility, 35 miles north of New York City. Although spokesman Donald Veno declined to comment on the move other than to say it was for "security reasons," rumors had reached the media concerning a relationship that Smart was allegedly conducting behind bars. Needless to say, her defense team was less than enthralled by the fact that they had not been told of the transfer beforehand. Commented one sarcastically, "There was a time in this country when prisoners had no rights."

—Colin Evans

A chance encounter at a Palm Beach, Florida, night spot between William Kennedy Smith and Patricia Bowman led to the couple returning to the Kennedy compound overlooking the Atlantic Ocean. From the house, they walked down to the beach. What happened next would become the subject of worldwide headlines. According to Bowman, Smith raped her. Smith maintained that everything that occurred had happened with Bowman's consent. The state, satisfied that Smith had a case to answer, filed rape charges against him.

When she rose to speak to a jury of four women and two men on December 2, 1991, Prosecutor Moira Lasch had already lost an important battle. Judge Mary Lupo had earlier denied the prosecution's request to admit the testimony of three other women who claimed that Smith had assaulted them between 1983 and 1988, on grounds that it did not demonstrate the discernible pattern of behavior required by Florida law for introduction. This meant that Lasch had to pin virtually her entire case on the word of the accuser.

First, though, Anne Mercer, a friend of Bowman's, who had also been at the Kennedy house on the night in question, told the court that Bowman was " . . . literally shaking and she looked messed up . . . she said she had been raped." When Mercer had confronted Smith to ask him how he could have acted so monstrously, his response, she said, was simply to shrug his shoulders.

In a blistering cross-examination, defense counsel Roy Black knocked gaping holes into Mercer's testimony. He forced a retreat from her earlier assertion to police that Bowman had been raped twice, and that on one of these occasions Smith's uncle, Senator Edward M. Kennedy of Massachusetts, had watched. Black also got Mercer to admit that she had failed to inform the authorities of details she subsequently revealed for the tabloid TV program *A Current Affair*. Gasps filled the courtroom when Mercer confessed that she had been paid $40,000 for her story. By implication, Black suggested that Mercer's tale had been heavily embellished for monetary gain. It was a stigma that the witness was never able to fully shrug off. Black drove home his advantage by playing Mercer a taped account she had made earlier for the police, which contained several discrepancies with the version she had provided the court.

T rial on TV or TV on trial? *Newsweek* reported that the William Kennedy Smith trial "put Court TV on the map" by providing gavel-to-gavel coverage, which left CNN "open to criticism for its frequent commercials."

In a surprise move, prosecutor Lasch produced the accuser early in the trial. To protect her identity, TV cameras obscured Bowman's face with a blue dot. (Following the trial, Bowman elected to abandon her anonymity for a television interview.) Referring to the defendant first as "Mr. Smith," and later as "that man," Bowman described the alleged assault, saying, "I thought he was going to kill me."

When Black chided Bowman for several lapses of memory, she insisted, "The only thing I can remember about that week is Mr. Smith raped me."

Black wasn't impressed and said, "I know you've been prepared to say that."

Bowman snapped back, "I have not been prepared to say anything."

Throughout his cross-examination, Black walked a fine line—undermining the accuser's credibility while trying not to appear bullying or insensitive. On those occasions when his questioning provoked a tearful response, Black would back off and suggest a recess. Under his probing, Bowman acknowledged a history of problems with men, resulting, she said, from "having one-night stands."

On rebuttal, Lasch asked Bowman whether she had any ulterior motives for bringing the charge. Bowman replied, "What he did to me was wrong. I have a child, and it's not right, and I don't want to live the rest of my life in fear of that man. And, I don't want to be responsible for him doing it to someone else."

This final comment brought Black to his feet, objecting. Judge Lupo ordered the remark stricken from the record, calling it inappropriate.

Curiously, the prosecution called Smith's uncle, Senator Kennedy, as its witness. If, as some observers believed, Lasch was attempting to visit some of the Senator's perceived foibles upon his nephew, then she sorely miscalculated. For some 40 minutes, Senator Kennedy managed to re-create Camelot in the Palm Beach Courthouse as he evoked memories of the family's numerous tragedies. Nothing he said was helpful to Lasch's case.

Much of the defense was built around high-priced forensic testimony. Charles M. Sieger, an architect, said that, given the house's construction, had Bowman screamed as she claimed, the sounds would have been clearly audible indoors, yet no resident admitted to hearing anything.

Jurors examine the clothing worn by alleged rape victim, Patricia Bowman, during the William Kennedy Smith trial on Friday, December 6, 1991. Lannis Waters/Palm Beach Post

Rather less successful was Professor Jay Siegel's testimony. He stated that sand found in Bowman's underwear most likely came from the beach, which tallied with Smith's version of events, and not the lawn, where Bowman claimed she had been raped. Lasch zeroed in. "Wouldn't you agree that a 6-foot-2, 200-pound man running up a beach is going to churn up some sand?" Siegel agreed. Lasch went on: "And if the defendant was wet . . . some of that [sand] could stick to his body, couldn't it?" Besides having to concede this possibility, Siegel was also forced to admit that the lawn itself actually contained a significant amount of sand, thus rendering his testimony virtually useless.

It took Smith just 29 minutes to tell his side of the story. Black concluded the brief account by asking if he had "at any time" raped his accuser. "No, I did not," Smith replied firmly.

Lasch went on the attack. "What are you saying, that she raped you, Mr. Smith?" Later, in reference to an alleged second sexual encounter, she leered, "What are you, some kind of sex machine?"

Smith weathered the assault coolly. He reiterated his story that the evening had turned ugly when he had inadvertently called the accuser Kathy. She "sort of snapped . . . she got very upset." According to Smith, Bowman later apologized as she was leaving the compound, "I am sorry I got upset . . . I had a wonderful night. You're a terrific guy." Smith said that minutes later she was back, crying and claiming that he had raped her, repeatedly calling him Michael.

Frustrated by Smith's matter-of-fact responses, Lasch adopted a different tack, claiming the Kennedy family was trying to engineer a cover-up. Smith would have none of it. "If you're implying that my family is lying to protect me, you are dead wrong." Judge Lupo was also less than impressed with this line of questioning: "If you ask one more question along these lines," she told Lasch, "you will not get away with it. Failure to abide by this instruction will result in legal action." It was a humiliating rebuke for the prosecutor, coming as it did with Judge Lupo's oblique reference to the fact that she suspected Lasch might be angling for a deliberate mistrial, which would salvage her case for another day.

In closing, Black said, "They want us to believe that this young man goes up there and rapes a screaming young woman under the open windows not only of his mother, but his sister, two

Charged with rape, William Kennedy Smith emerges from the courtroom during his December 1991 trial, where a crowd of young women voice their support.

prosecutors from New York, and the father of one of them who is a former special agent for the FBI!" Making no attempt to apologize for his client's self-confessed dishonorable behavior on the night concerned, Black still appealed to the jury to exhibit "general, human common sense."

Lasch could dwell only on inconsistencies. Referring to Bowman, "She didn't know this man. She didn't even have an opportunity to know him . . . This woman has had a child. She's a high-risk pregnancy. If she was going to have consensual sex on March 30, 1991, she would use birth control."

On December 11, 1991, the case went to the jury. After deliberating for only 77 minutes, it returned with a verdict of not guilty.

Millions of viewers watched this drama play out on television. For many, it was their first glimpse of the extraordinary problems that attend "date rape" cases—cases that may well hinge on one person's word against another's. Courtroom demeanor usually carries the day.

After gaining his medical degree from Georgetown University, Smith began a residency at the University of New Mexico Medical School. But controversy continued to plague him. On Saturday, October 23, 1993, the police were called to a brawl outside Bardo, a bar in Arlington, Virginia. When they arrived at around 1:45 A.M., they found Smith with blood on his face. The club bouncer, Henry C. Cochran, had also suffered facial cuts, but declined medical treatment. Through his lawyer, Gregory Craig, Smith explained how he and his friends had been harangued by a group of people in the bar, the most offensive of whom then sat down at Smith's table and began making derogatory comments about the Florida rape trial. As tempers flared, the argument moved outside, where Smith saw the man who had harassed him talking to another, larger man. Unknown to Smith, that man was the club bouncer. A fistfight broke out. According to the bar manager, Andy Stewart, Smith was "totally apologetic and acted as if it was a big mistake."

Arrested on a charge of assault and battery, Smith was ordered to stand trial on December 3, 1993. Following the postponement of that hearing it was announced on July 27, 1994, that Smith and Cochran had settled out of court.

In April 1995, Smith was still doing his residency at New Mexico.

—Colin Evans

For several weeks following the January 15, 1989, shooting of Betty Jeanne Solomon in her Westchester County, New York, home, husband Paul Solomon was the chief suspect. But when police learned that Paul Solomon's longtime lover, Carolyn Warmus, had been more relentless than ever in her pursuit of the reluctant widower, attention turned to the 27-year-old Manhattan schoolteacher. The investigation revealed a woman with a turbulent history of romantic fixations, most often with unavailable men. There was evidence, too—enough to warrant a murder indictment against Warmus. Guaranteed immunity from prosecution, Solomon agreed to testify against his former lover when her trial began on January 14, 1991.

In his opening statement, Chief Prosecutor James A. McCarty described Warmus as driven by a "consuming passion to possess" Solomon. McCarty conceded the lack of any single piece of proof that would, on its own, prove Warmus guilty, but "like pieces of a puzzle," he said, circumstantial evidence would "reveal a clear picture of the killer . . . Carolyn Warmus."

David L. Lewis, lawyer for the defendant, countered that his client was the victim of a "deliberate, malicious" frame-up, reminding the jury that "love and passion are not on trial here. This is a trial about murder."

Carolyn Warmus takes a moment to look back at the crowd attending her murder trial at the Westchester County Courthouse in White Plains, New York, on January 23, 1991. The ex-school teacher was charged with shooting Betty Jeanne Solomon, the wife of Warmus's former lover, Paul Solomon. AP/Wide World Photos

The first witness to link Warmus to a potential murder weapon was Private Investigator James A. Russo. In the fall of 1988, Warmus had come to him, he said, seeking protection from Betty Jeanne Solomon who was jealous of the defendant's affair with her husband. Russo had suggested a bodyguard. "Her answer was no," he said. "I pushed her to say exactly what she wanted. She said a 'machine gun and silencer,' I said, 'We're not arms dealers.'"

When Paul Solomon took the stand, he cataloged a bizarre marriage. While acknowledging that neither partner had been faithful and there had been "ups and downs," he maintained that the union was basically sound. Responding to questions about his affair with Warmus, Solomon said that for some time he had been trying unsuccessfully to terminate the relationship. Even so, he admitted meeting Warmus on the night of the killing and having sex with her in a car. Afterwards he had gone home and found his wife murdered. Unnerved by Warmus's subsequent and, he said, unwanted pestering, he confronted her in a bar. "Did you have anything to do with Betty Jeanne's death?" he asked. She replied, ".No."

For five days Solomon underwent a merciless battering at the hands of Defense Counsel Lewis, who insinuated that it was actually Solomon himself who had arranged the murder. "You told your wife you'd be home early, but you didn't come home early because you knew your wife was dead!"

Finally, Solomon erupted. "You twist and turn words, manipulate facts . . . to make them what they aren't," he shouted. But Lewis scored heavily when he drew an admission from the witness that he stood to profit significantly from his wife's death, having already signed a movie contract worth $175,000.

ANOTHER PRIVATE EYE TAKES THE STAND

The star prosecution witness was yet another private investigator, Vincent Parco. He testified that one week before the shooting, he had sold Warmus a .25-caliber pistol, the kind used to kill Betty Jeanne Solomon, equipped with a silencer. (The murder weapon was never found.) Parco claimed he had only done so after considerable badgering by the defendant. "Almost every time I'd see her, she'd bring it up." The silencer had been his idea, so she could practice in a "house, woods or garage, and no one would know."

News stories during the trial dug into Warmus's past to find a history of instability: Court papers showed that while she was a student at the University of Michigan, she had become obsessed with a graduate student with whom she had had a relationship, aggressively pursuing him and his fiancée until they finally got a restraining order against her.

Lewis launched an assault on Parco's credibility, forcing him to admit his own infatuation with Warmus, and asserting, without producing evidence, that it was Parco, hired by Paul Solomon, who had shot Betty Jeanne Solomon and then framed Warmus.

Strong circumstantial evidence tying Warmus to the murder came in the form of phone company records, which showed that the defendant had called a New Jersey sporting goods shop on the day of the killing. The prosecution alleged that, using a fake ID card, Warmus bought some .25-caliber bullets from the store, then she shot Betty Jeanne Solomon nine times, before keeping her rendezvous with Paul Solomon.

In response, the defense produced its own phone record. Not only did this record not show the call to New Jersey, but it also logged an additional 6:44 P.M. call from Warmus's Manhattan apartment: if she has made that call, it would have been virtually impossible for her to have committed the murder several miles away at 7:15 P.M. But the veracity of this second record was seriously challenged by MCI executive Thomas Sabol, who declared it a forgery.

Warmus had a privileged—but perhaps not an all-too happy—upbringing in suburban Detroit. In February 1990, *People* magazine reported having interviewed her former peers from Birmingham Seaholm High School, who described her as hungry for affection and remembered her as someone who tried to "buy friends."

With Warmus exercising her right to silence, the major defense witness was Joseph Lisella, a building contractor. He claimed to have overheard a conversation, allegedly between a "Parco" and a "Solomon" in a Yonkers, New York, bowling alley bathroom less than an hour after the killing. Lisella said "Paul" had handed over $20,000 to the other man, saying, "Count it if you don't believe me." Later "Vinnie" had remarked, "Don't worry about the gun. It's in the deepest part of the river."

During cross-examination McCarty attempted to impugn Lisella's credibility by outlining several house fires connected with the witness. Lisella denied McCarty's charge that "people call you 'Toaster Joe,'" but did admit to contact with Warmus's father, Thomas, the multi-millionaire owner of a Michigan life insurance company.

THE JURY DEADLOCKS

Following directions from Judge John Carey, the jurors retired to consider their verdict. Twelve days later, they announced themselves deadlocked, and a mistrial was declared.

On January 22, 1992, the state tried again. This time Warmus's defense was in the hands of William I. Aronwald, a somewhat more understated advocate than his predecessor. He had the same evidence to deal with, except for one important difference: Original crime scene photographs had shown a black, bloodstained glove near the body. Somehow it had vanished, only to reappear between trials when Paul Solomon was searching through a box in his bedroom closet.

From Warmus's credit card records, the prosecution was able to prove that the defendant had purchased just such a pair of gloves one year before the murder. Aronwald fumed, accusing McCarty of "trial by ambush," but the evidence was in and its effect was deadly, especially when forensic expert Dr. Peter DeForest gave his opinion that stains on the glove could be human blood.

Again it was no easy matter for the jury, but after a week of deliberation, it convicted Warmus of murder. On June 26, 1992, Judge Carey passed sentence, 25 years-to-life, and the blond-haired defendant was led away without uttering a word in her own defense.

WAS KEY EVIDENCE SUPPRESSED?

On March 15, 1993, Aronwald filed a motion to set aside the conviction on grounds that two key pieces of evidence had been deliberately suppressed by the prosecution. The state, he said, knew that Paul Solomon was having an affair with another woman, Barbara Bailor, three months before his wife was murdered. He also claimed that two gloves, not one, had been found at the crime scene. The second glove, which according to Aronwald could have acquitted Warmus, had been found outside the apartment building and had now been mislaid by the prosecution.

The hearing to consider this application began on May 18, 1993, and featured yet another private detective, Anthony Souza, a retired Yonkers, New York, police officer. He testified to the existence of the affair between Solomon and Bailor, and he claimed that he had been hired by Bailor to spy on Betty Jean Solomon. A supposed file on the surveillance, allegedly given to the prosecution, was now missing. If the intent was to suggest that Bailor and Solomon had somehow connived at murder, then Prosecutor Steven Bender was unimpressed. "Have you ever represented yourself to be someone you're not?" he asked the witness. "Sure," replied Souza. "I did that when I worked for the police, and your office, too." Such glibness and a missing glove, the very existence of which was impossible to prove, hardly made for a formidable case, and it was no surprise when Judge Carey refused the application.

Again Carolyn Warmus was a mute spectator to all of this, her only contribution being a series of hastily scribbled notes which she passed to her attorney. She continues to serve her sentence.

—Colin Evans

Navy Lieutenant Paula Coughlin was a 30-year-old helicopter pilot when she went to the annual convention of the Tailhook Association at the Las Vegas, Nevada, Hilton Hotel in September 1991. Tailhook was a private organization of active and retired Navy and Marine Corps fliers. Its name came from a device at the rear of a Navy plane that hooks onto a braking cable on the flight deck of an aircraft carrier as the plane lands.

After the weekend convention, Lieutenant Coughlin filed an official complaint, through Navy channels, saying that she had been sexually abused when she found herself "running a gauntlet" of dozens of officers with groping hands in a third-floor corridor of the hotel. At the same time, the Las Vegas Hilton billed the Navy for $23,000 worth of damages suffered during Tailhook's wild party.

With the whistle blown, the Navy announced, on October 30, that it was breaking all ties with Tailhook. It began looking into similar allegations made by several other women.

Seven months later, on May 1, 1992, separate reports were made public by the Naval Investigative Service and the Navy Inspector General. More than 1,500 people who had attended the convention had been interviewed. Fourteen female naval officers and 12 female civilians reported sexual abuse. The convention was described as a beehive of hospitality suites in which alcohol was heavily consumed while the cavorting of nude exotic dancers was punctuated by the screening of pornographic films. Navy Secretary H. Lawrence Garrett III immediately ordered the Navy and Marine Corps to begin disciplinary action against nearly 70 officers, including six who were accused of obstructing the inquiries and 57 suspected of participating in the "gauntlet."

Shortly thereafter, a supplemental report revealed that Secretary Garrett, himself, had been seen in one of the hospitality suites where the scandalous activities had occurred. The Defense Department's Inspector General took over the investigation, Tailhook canceled its 1992 convention, and Admiral Frank B. Kelso, Chief of Naval Operations, promised a service-wide program to train Navy personnel about sexual harassment issues. Admiral Kelso also admitted that he had attended the 1991 convention, but said he "didn't see anything untoward."

THE PRESIDENT IS BRIEFED ON THE SITUATION

It was not until June 26, 1992, that Defense Secretary Richard B. Cheney briefed President George Bush on the reports. The President invited Lieutenant Coughlin to the White House that day to hear her description of an experience she said left her "the most frightened I've ever been." Within hours, Secretary Garrett resigned. Accepting the resignation that evening, the President did not include the "thank you" usually given a high official who resigns. Three days later, the Appropriations Committee of the U.S. House of Representatives, protesting the "arrogance and obstruction" of the Navy, cut from its defense spending bill the funds for some 10,000 active-duty administrative personnel, and the Armed Services Committee of the U.S. Senate blocked the approval of nearly 4,500 Navy and Marine promotions and transfers.

On July 29 the *Los Angeles Times* reported that aviators at the Miramar Naval Air Station near San Diego, California, had turned over to the Defense Department Inspector General's Office five rolls of film showing a teenage girl, apparently drunk, being stripped of her clothing by a crowd of rowdy Navy and Marine fliers in the gauntlet corridor at the 1991 Las Vegas Tailhook convention.

The next day, the U.S. House of Representatives Armed Services Committee held a hearing on discrimination against women in the military. Four members of the Joint Chiefs of Staff testified.

Admiral Kelso, Chief of Naval Operations, admitted that the Navy had not paid attention to earlier evidence that women in the service were being mistreated.

On April 23, 1993, Pentagon Inspector General Derek J. Vander Schaaf released the Defense Department's three-hundred-page report on the Tailhook convention. Among the subheads of chapters in the report were "Streaking," "Mooning," "Butt Biting," "Pornography," "Public and Paid Sex," and "Ballwalking." Citing "the culmination of a long-term failure of leadership in naval aviation," it said that 117 officers were "implicated in one or more incidents of indecent assault, indecent exposure, conduct unbecoming an officer or failure to act in a proper leadership capacity." Of the 117 officers, the report stated that 23 were involved in indecent assaults and 23 in indecent exposure, while 51 lied to investigators. All faced disciplinary action. In addition, the report concluded that "the number of individuals involved in all types of misconduct or other inappropriate behavior" was "more widespread than these figures would suggest." Altogether, it said, several hundred officers concealed information so that "collective 'stonewalling' significantly increased the difficulty of the investigation."

REPORT CITES 90 VICTIMS

The 90 victims of assault included 7 servicemen, 49 civilian women, 22 servicewomen, 6 government employees, and the wives of 6 conventioneers. According to the report, misbehavior was traditional in "a type of 'free-fire zone'" at the convention, with the fliers acting "indiscriminately and without fear of censure or retribution in matters of sexual conduct and drunkenness." Furthermore, it noted, previous conventions and the triumphs of the Persian Gulf War earlier in 1991 had set up a sort of "can you top this" atmosphere at the convention.

The Navy temporarily reassigned six senior officers (all captains and commanders) to desk duty ashore, but it took no disciplinary action against them, while Vice Admiral J. Paul Reason, commander of the Atlantic surface fleet, reviewed the report. A week later, the admiral docked $1,000 from the pay of each of 10 officers—1 lieutenant commander, 2 junior-grade lieutenants, and 7 lieutenants—and gave them letters of admonition.

In a pre-trial hearing in a Marine courtroom in Quantico, Virginia, on August 17, 1993, Lieutenant Coughlin faced Captain Gregory Bonam, the pilot she had recognized, both from a photograph and in a lineup, as her chief molester in the gauntlet. Bonam's lawyer produced a photograph, purportedly snapped the night of the gauntlet, that showed him wearing not the burnt orange T-shirt that Coughlin had sworn she saw him in but a shirt with green and black stripes. No witness testified as to when the picture was taken. Character witnesses backed him as "very moral" and a "very good person." The Marine judge saw no need for a trial.

Six months later, in February 1994, after examining 140 cases of misconduct, the Navy closed the investigation of Tailhook. After a pre-trial hearing, Captain William T. Vest, Jr., a Navy judge, ruled that Admiral Kelso had used his influence as Chief of Naval Operations "in a manner designed to shield his personal involvement in Tailhook." Under oath, the admiral and three of his aides had testified that he did not witness the gauntlet assaults and that he was nowhere near them. But, said Vest, testimony of more than a dozen witnesses proved that the admiral—despite his denial—was present at some of Tailhook's wildest parties and made no effort to stop the sexual assaults. Furthermore, Vest added, Tailhook's reputation for including prostitutes, strippers, porn films, and plenty of alcohol in its festivities should have alerted the admiral that there might be trouble. Having put the blame on Admiral Kelso's shoulders, Vest concluded that charges against three of Kelso's subordinates should be dropped. Since Kelso's retirement was imminent further action was not taken. No trial followed the pre-trial hearing.

While in Vegas, Tailhook attendees could have:

- caught Dean Martin performing at Bally's;
- laughed at David Brenner's comedy at the Golden Nugget;
- grooved to the tunes of the Temptations and the Four Tops—at the Hilton;
- listened to Liza Minnelli sing at the Riviera.

The U.S. Senate has the responsibility of approving the retirement rank and pensions of top military officers. By law, Admiral Kelso was entitled to retire with a two-star rank and a $67,000 annual pension. But, following tradition, the Senate's Armed Services Committee voted him four stars and $81,000 a year. For the

full Senate's vote on April 19, nine Congresswomen, led by Representative Pat Schroeder (D-Colo.), marched onto the Senate floor to
join the seven female Senators (five Democrats and two Republicans) who opposed the committee's recommendation. The vote was
54 to 43 in favor of Kelso.

COUGHLIN SUES HILTON

With the investigation closed, Lieutenant Paula Coughlin
sued both the Tailhook Association and the Las Vegas Hilton for
compensatory damages for emotional distress. Then, citing emotional stress brought on by the lawsuits, and writing that "the covert
attacks on me that followed have stripped me of my ability to
serve," she resigned from the Navy on February 7, 1994. Her resignation letter made note of a newsletter titled *The Gauntlet* put out
by former Navy pilots who used the pseudonym, "Paul A. Coffin."

On September 8, 1994, the Tailhook Association settled for
an undisclosed amount. Four days later, the Hilton suit opened in
the Las Vegas courtroom of Judge Philip M. Pro of the Federal District Court before a jury of four men and four women.

During a seven-week trial, Coughlin accused the Hilton
Hotels Corporation and its subsidiaries of failing to set up proper
security for the Tailhook convention, despite the fact that they had
hosted 19 earlier Tailhooks, at many of which drunkenness and
debauchery had been exhibited. Witnesses testified that during at
least one convention, Hilton security guards found a teenage girl, in
a Tailhook hospitality suite, nude from the waist down while in a
drunken stupor.

Coughlin's lead lawyer, Dennis Schoville, argued that Tailhook had changed his client's life by bringing on a serious post-
traumatic stress disorder. Testimony by psychiatrists and psychologists on both sides observed that she was deeply depressed and
Coughlin herself testified that she had become suicidal as a result of
the Las Vegas experience.

Hilton Defense Attorney Eugene Walt, however, produced a
deposition made in August 1993 by Navy Lieutenant Roland Diaz
that said Lieutenant Coughlin had allowed him to shave her legs
while she was in uniform the night before she was assaulted in the
gauntlet. Coughlin emphatically denied the allegation. Her attorney
commented that the Diaz testimony was a setup and that the

defense lawyers would do almost anything to win, including "destroying her reputation."

Walt admitted that the gauntlet incident had occurred but said it was over-dramatized, and he argued that the post-traumatic stress "appears to be mild and closer to anger and less to a victim who has been sexually molested." Attorney Schoville ridiculed Walt's use of the word "mild," saying, "She feels used and dirty," and implored the jury to award his client $5–$10 million in damages.

As Coughlin ended her testimony, Attorney Walt questioned why she had resigned from the Navy after agreeing in April 1992 to re-enlist for at least six years, enabling her to earn a bonus of $60,750. "I was drummed out of the Navy," she replied.

Former Navy Lt. Paula Coughlin (r) prepares to enter the U.S. District Courthouse in Las Vegas on Monday, September 12, 1994, for the beginning session of the Tailhook trial. Coughlin sued the Las Vegas Hilton and Hilton Hotels Corporation for failing to prevent alleged sexual assaults during the 1991 convention of Naval and Marine aviators, held at the resort. In October 1994, the jury found the Las Vegas Hilton negligent and awarded Coughlin $1.7 million in compensatory damages. In 1995, a federal judge reduced the award to $1.3 million. AP/Wide World Photos

On October 28, 1994, its second day of deliberation, the jury found the Las Vegas Hilton negligent in failing to provide adequate security during the 1991 Tailhook convention. It awarded the former Navy lieutenant $1.7 million in compensatory damages for emotional distress and $5 million in punitive damages.

Almost six months later, on March 9, 1995, Judge Pro reduced the award. Revealing that the Tailhook Association's settlement, which had not been disclosed in September, was $400,000, the judge ruled that the amount must be subtracted from the $1.7

million compensatory-damages award. Furthermore, citing Nevada law that limits punitive damages to three times compensatory damages, Judge Pro cut the punitive award to $3.9 million. Thus Coughlin's total award stood at $5.2 million. The Las Vegas Hilton and its parent, the Hilton Hotels Corporation, however, are still appealing the judgment.

—Bernard Ryan, Jr.

At age 25, Mike Tyson had already won and lost the world heavyweight boxing championship. Seemingly on the verge of challenging to regain his crown, in July 1991, he attended the Black Expo in Indianapolis, Indiana. One of the scheduled events was the Miss Black America Pageant, and one of the contestants was Desiree Washington, 18-year-old Miss Rhode Island. Tyson, whose fondness for and occasional problems with attractive young women were well-documented, invited Washington to his hotel room. Around 2 A.M. on July 19, she agreed. Three days later Washington went to the police. What she had to say resulted in Tyson facing charges of rape and related offenses.

Once the jury was empaneled on January 29, 1992, and after Judge Patricia J. Gifford had denied a request from Tyson's chief attorney, Vincent J. Fuller, that the accuser's sexual history be admitted into evidence, it was time for the opening statements.

In the Indianapolis courtroom Prosecutor J. Gregory Garrison delivered a ringing indictment of the defendant. "This man," he said pointing to Tyson, "is guilty of pinning that 18-year-old girl to a bed and confining her . . . callously and maliciously raping her even though she cried out in pain."

Fuller, on the other hand, depicted a calculating vixen "mature beyond her 18 years," sophisticated and poised and out for money, an educated overachiever more than a match for a high school dropout like Tyson. To be sure, Washington's level of sophistication had unnerved prosecutors before the trial, but when it came time for her to testify, she did so in a naive, childlike voice, peppering her speech with expressions like "yucky."

She described receiving a phone call from Tyson at 1:36 A.M. Minutes later, believing herself to be en route to a party, she joined Tyson in his limousine. As soon as she entered the car, Tyson grabbed her. Washington testified, "I kind of jumped back because I was surprised that, being who he is, he acted like that and, besides, his breath smelled kind of bad."

Instead of the expected party, they drove to Tyson's hotel. Once inside his room, Tyson resumed his advances. At that point, Washington said, she told him that she was "not like the girls he must be used to hanging out with." She went on to say that Tyson, undeterred, pinned her down on the bed with one arm and used his free hand to undress her. All the while, she said, he mocked her efforts to resist, saying, "Don't fight me. Don't fight me."

Then the alleged rape took place. Washington described the pain as "excruciating," and that when she began to cry, "he started laughing like it was a game or something, like it was funny." Then she ran from the room, shoes in hand. Outside she saw Tyson's chauffeur who offered to drive her back to her hotel.

When cross-examined, Washington conceded that on several occasions she had had the opportunity to leave the hotel room but chose not to do so. Fuller probed reports that after meeting Tyson, she had told other pageant contestants, "He's rich. Did you see what Robin Givens [Tyson's ex-wife] got out of him? Besides, he's dumb." Washington denied that any such exchange had ever taken place. Neither had she sung, "Money, money, money, money, money," from the song "For the Love of Money" to a girlfriend later, as alleged.

Partial corroboration of Washington's story came from the chauffeur, Virginia Foster, 44. When Washington returned to the limousine, said Foster, "She looked like she may have been in a state of shock . . . dazed, disoriented. She seemed scared." (Earlier the defense had successfully petitioned to have disallowed as evi-

Mike Tyson leaves the City-County Building in downtown Indianapolis after his pre-sentence hearing with probation officials in February 1992. Mary Ann Carter

dence Foster's claim that Tyson had been sexually aggressive toward her also. No charges were ever filed.)

Dr. Thomas Richardson, the emergency room physician who examined Washington more than 24 hours after the incident, confirmed the presence of abrasions "consistent with forced or very hard intercourse."

Earlier prosecution comparisons between Tyson's menacing bulk and Washington's slight 98-pound stature came into stark relief as the defendant took the stand. He began by saying that everything had taken place with Washington's full cooperation and consent. Asked by Fuller if he forced himself upon her, Tyson replied, "No, I didn't. I didn't violate her in any way, sir."

In graphic terms, Tyson described the encounter, but denied Garrison's claims that he had willfully misled Washington, insisting she had been aware of his sexual intentions beforehand and had only become annoyed when he remained in bed afterwards and refused to accompany her downstairs. "I told her that was the way it was. I said 'The limousine is downstairs. If you don't want to use the limousine, you can walk.'"

Quizzed by Garrison on why he had urged Washington to wear loose-fitting clothes, Tyson admitted that he had planned to have sex in the limousine and tight-fitting jeans "would have complicated it."

Ten hours of jury deliberation produced a guilty verdict. On March 26, 1992, Judge Gifford passed sentence: ten years imprisonment, with the last four suspended.

Often, in trial by jury, demeanor is everything. In the words of Deputy Defense Counsel Barbara Trathen, Desiree Washington made "a great victim" on the stand, demure, almost adolescent. By contrast, Tyson's untutored responses to questioning came across as brutish and arrogant.

After learning on March 7, 1994, that the Supreme Court had refused to hear his appeal, Tyson applied to the Indianapolis Parole Board. On June 13, 1994, a hearing was convened to consider the application. His lawyers, arguing that their client was a rehabilitated man, produced three witnesses who testified that Tyson's attitude behind bars had undergone a change. Under cross-examination, however, all three said they had never heard Tyson admit to raping Washington. Tyson, himself, was oddly belligerent on this point when questioned. "I do not take responsibility for rap-

An *Esquire* profile of Tyson in 1988 gives an eerie characterization of the fighter, considering what was to come. Two British reporters comment on accusations that Tyson is gay. "Ridiculous," claims one, "Tyson is the ultimate heterosexual." The other responds with "if there's a *Guiness Book of World Records* category for, you know, gals, I think the record is in jeopardy with Mike Tyson. . . . The gals line up around the block."

ing anyone," he told the court. "I have done no criminal conduct. The jury said I did."

It was an attitude that cut little ice with Judge Gifford, who had presided over Tyson's trial. "I have not heard what I wanted to hear," she said, also noting that Tyson had failed to meet the legal requirement of completing an educational or vocational course while in prison, which defense lawyers attributed to the constant stream of visitors that made it difficult for Tyson to concentrate. In her summing-up, the judge said that she wanted Tyson to acknowledge his "inexcusable conduct." Without that, she was unprepared to grant his parole request.

Amid rumors of financial problems—Tyson had cashed in his sole remaining life insurance policy to fund his legal campaign—it was announced on November 7, 1994, that he had withdrawn an appeal to have his conviction overturned.

But on the morning of March 25, 1995, Tyson was freed from the Indiana Youth Center where he had served three years of his six-year sentence. Parole had been granted based on his in-prison activities, which had recently included reading, converting to Islam, working out, and shedding 30 pounds. Upon his release Tyson made no public comments but a statement from him said, "I'm very happy to be out and on my way home. I want to thank everyone for their support. I will have more to say in the future. I'll see you all soon." His first stop was to pray at a mosque, where he was joined by boxing great Muhammad Ali, among others. Tyson's fans and supporters remained eager to see the former heavyweight champ return to the ring. And there is a compelling financial reason for Tyson to return to the ring. The boxer earned at least $16 million during his last full year of boxing, but at the time he went to trial, his assets were reported to be down to $5 million. After three years in prison, that amount was thought to be severely depleted. Not to worry: On August 19, 1995, Tyson entered the ring again and in 89 seconds defeated his opponent, Peter McNeeley, to win an estimated prize of $25 million.

Desiree Washington, who reportedly found it difficult returning to a normal life after the traumatic events, graduated from college in spring 1995.

—Colin Evans

n October 12, 1990, the television program, *America's Most Wanted* broadcast a segment on Lawrencia Ann "Bambi" Bembenek, a Milwaukee, Wisconsin, woman who had been convicted of murder in 1981. She had escaped in July 1990 from Taycheedah Correctional Institute, Wisconsin's prison for women. A California viewer called the FBI. The photograph on TV, he reported, looked like the waitress who had served him recently at the Columbia Grill & Tavern in Thunder Bay, Ontario, Canada.

At the Columbia Grill on October 17, Thunder Bay Police Detective Ron Arthur compared the attractive 132-pound, 5'10", 32-year-old waitress called Jennifer Gazzano with the blurred photo faxed from the FBI. He told her she was "not the person we want," and departed.

Jennifer hurried to the apartment where she lived with a short-order cook called Anthony Gazzano. Within the hour, detectives knocked. "The game is over," they told Bembenek. "We know who you are." Detective Arthur had played for time while he checked into the American waitress's lack of legal papers required to work in Canada. The couple, who were hastily packing when the police arrived, were jailed immediately.

"Anthony Gazzano" is 34-year-old Dominick Gugliatto, a divorced father of three whose sister, a prison-mate of Bembenek's, had introduced him to the convicted murderer. During his prison visits, they had fallen in love and became engaged to be married. On the July day when Bembenek disappeared through the window of the prison's laundry room, Nick Gugliatto had also vanished from Milwaukee.

In jail in Thunder Bay, the couple expected to be deported. But the deportation hearing resulted only in a Canadian attorney being assigned to Bembenek's case. Researching her story, he told her she might be able to claim refugee status.

The lawyer also learned that on January 30, 1981, Bembenek, then a Playboy Club hostess, had married Elfred O. "Fred" Schultz, Jr., a 32-year-old Milwaukee police detective. At the time, she was 21 years old and three months earlier had been fired as a Milwaukee police officer on suspicion of smoking marijuana. She had gained the resentment of many policemen by filing a sex discrimination charge over her dismissal. Schultz had divorced his first wife only three months before he married Bembenek.

Bambi had lots of fans in Thunder Bay, where her former landlord described her as "a lovely woman—kind, warm, and outgoing," her former employer called her "so polite, never lost her temper," and a friend remarked that "people who knew her seemed to think a lot of her."

—*Maclean's,* October 29, 1990

Schultz and his first wife, Christine, 30, had two sons—Sean, 11, and Shannon, 7. Since the divorce, Schultz had been ordered by the court to stay away from Christine and the house he had built for her. She had changed the locks and had told her lawyer she was afraid Schultz might kill her.

THE 1981 MURDER

On May 27, 1981, at 2 A.M., Sean Schultz awakened when he felt something—he couldn't tell whether it was a rope or a wire—tightening around his neck. A big, gloved hand covered his eyes, nose, and mouth. He screamed, waking his brother. Shannon leapt up and kicked the intruder—a big man wearing a green army jacket. As the intruder ran across the hall into their mother's room, Shannon noticed his red pony tail. The terrified boys stood frozen. A woman's voice said, "God, please don't do that." Then the boys heard a sound like a firecracker. They ran into their mother's room. The man was gone. Their mother had been murdered.

Fred Schultz was on duty that night. He called Bembenek at 2:42 A.M. to tell her Christine had been killed. At 5 A.M., he returned home, accompanied by Michael Durfee, his partner. They hurried to the bedroom. Bembenek followed, finding Durfee emptying Fred's off-duty .38-caliber revolver and sniffing the barrel. "Nope," he said, "this gun hasn't been fired."

"I just wanted to check out this gun right away and make our report on it," said Fred.

Judy Zess, who had once roomed with Bembenek and who was also a former Milwaukee cop, told police that Bembenek had talked of having Christine killed. A reddish-brown wig was found flushed down a toilet in the apartment complex where Schultz and Bembenek lived. The police went to Milwaukee County District Attorney E. Michael McCann. The murderer, they told him, had to be Bembenek.

A few days later, detectives asked Bembenek to take a polygraph test. They said they were also asking Schultz and Zess to take one as well. Bembenek had just applied for a job as a security officer at Marquette University and had already been put through a long and exhausting lie detector test. From her police work, she knew the tests were not always conclusive. She refused to take the test but Schultz agreed to one.

The next day, Schultz's lawyer called Bembenek to tell her that the police crime lab had discovered blood on Schultz's service revolver. When he came home, he said, "They might as well be accusing me, but I was on duty that night. Then they were ridiculous enough to suggest that you might have been able to switch guns that night."

"Me?" asked Bembenek.

"You didn't have an alibi that night. I passed the polygraph, and you refused to take one."

BAMBI MAINTAINS SHE'S INNOCENT

On June 24, 1981, Bembenek was arrested for first-degree murder in the death of Christine Schultz. The media in America and over-

Lawrencia "Bambi" Bembenek on the witness stand during her first-degree murder trial in Milwaukee, Wisconsin, on March 5, 1982. Bembenek was charged with the murder of Christine Schultz, her husband Fred's first wife.
AP/Wide World Photos

seas had a field day. The sensational stories described a Playboy Bunny killer, an ex-model with great legs, blue eyes, and blond hair. Headlines read, "Ex-cop kills ex-wife of cop husband." Bembenek pleaded not guilty.

At the preliminary hearing, Zess testified that Bembenek had talked about having Christine "blown away." Zess also said she had seen a green jogging suit in Bembenek's apartment. Bembenek testified she owned no green clothing. She denied any talk of killing Christine. Her husband took the Fifth Amendment. Judge Ralph Adam Fine granted him immunity for testifying as a government witness. Finally, the judge said the case was "the most circumstantial" he had ever seen. "Yet there is a link of probable cause," he went on, "between defendant and the death of Christine Schultz. That link is, of course, Fred Schultz's off-duty gun. According to the ballistics report, the bullet recovered from the body of Christine Schultz was fired from that gun." The judge ordered Bembenek to stand trial.

On February 22, 1982, Circuit Court Judge Michael Skwierawski's 144-seat courtroom was packed. Downtown Milwaukee throbbed with the pulse of reporters and spectators eager for every sensational detail. Television beamed the trial into every living room. Outlining the state's case, Assistant District Attorney Robert Kraemer told the jury that Bembenek "brutally murdered Christine Schultz" although she intended only to scare Christine into moving out of the house in order to relieve Schultz of a money problem.

No witness testified that Bembenek was outside her apartment on the night of the murder. But both Schultz's off-duty revolver and his keys to Christine's house had been at home with Bembenek while he was on duty. Witnesses said they had seen her in the past in a green jogging suit. Synthetic hair recovered from Christine's leg matched fibers of the wig flushed down the toilet in Bembenek's building.

Zess, a key state witness, admitted she had been fired as a police officer, was the girlfriend of a convicted drug dealer, and had a key to Bembenek's apartment. It was alleged that she could have planted the wig and the murder weapon. No one could swear that the gun inspected by Detective Durfee just after the murder was the same gun Schultz turned over to the crime lab. And Sean Schultz insisted that the person who throttled him and killed his mother could not have been Bembenek.

BEMBENEK IS SENT TO PRISON

The jury deliberated for three and a half days and found Lawrencia Bembenek guilty of first-degree manslaughter. On March 9, 1982, she was sentenced to life imprisonment. In February 1983, the Wisconsin Court of Appeals upheld the conviction. In June 1984, Bembenek filed for divorce. While she was in prison, she researched her case in the prison library. She tried to get her lawyer, Donald S. Eisenberg, to tell her why the perjury of Zess had not been exposed during the trial or why no one had carefully checked out Schultz's alibi for the night of the murder. Then she learned that Eisenberg was being disbarred as a result of another case.

Over her years in prison, Bembenek took correspondence courses from the University of Wisconsin, maintaining a top-notch grade-point average for four years. When she met Nick Gugliatto in 1990, she was one class requirement short of a bachelor's degree.

On May 6, 1992, an exhibit of 23 of Bembenek's paintings opened at the University of Wisconsin in Milwaukee. *USA Today* called it "the latest evidence in the folkloric status of Bembenek, whose conviction and subsequent escape from jail prompted several books, a stage play, a popular song, a sandwich, and three . . . television movies."

On June 20, 1990, the Wisconsin Court of Appeals, releasing an 18-page decision, again turned down Bembenek's request for a new trial. By then she had served eight years in prison. When she saw an opportunity to scramble out of the prison laundry room, she took it.

"RUN, BAMBI, RUN!"

Many Wisconsinites cheered her escape. Bumper stickers and T-shirts read, "Run, Bambi, Run!" A bar held a Bembenek look-alike contest. Lunch counters sold "Bembenek Burgers." On a radio talk show, 72 percent of callers said they wouldn't turn her in. But *America's Most Wanted* returned Bembenek to prison.

With her claim for refugee status clogged in the Canadian court system, Bembenek decided on February 29, 1992, to return to the United States. Former Federal Prosecutor Sheldon Zenner had taken her case without pay and early in 1992 he had convinced the Milwaukee Circuit Court to hold a John Doe investigation—a formal inquiry to determine whether a crime had been committed. Zenner filed a 147-page brief that included testimony from five forensic experts stating that the gun in evidence at the trial could not have been the murder weapon. Prosecutors agreed to let Bembenek plead "no contest" to a charge of second-degree murder, a lesser charge that carried a 20-year sentence. On December 9, 1992, Judge Skwierawski, who had presided over Bembenek's trial in 1982, released her on parole based on time already served.

On December 20, 1992, Bembenek received a B.A. degree from the University of Wisconsin. She then wrote her autobiography, *Woman on Trial.* She never married Nick Gugliatto, who was sentenced to a year in jail for helping her escape. Her ex-husband left the Milwaukee police force, moved to Florida, remarried, and set up his own contracting business. Sean moved in with his father. Shannon lives with his mother's sister.

—Bernard Ryan, Jr.

AMY FISHER AND JOEY BUTTAFUOCO CASES

One sunny May afternoon in 1992, Mary Jo Buttafuoco found a teen-aged girl ringing the doorbell of her suburban Massapequa, New York, home. The girl accused Buttafuoco's 36-year-old husband Joey of having an affair with her younger sister. Unimpressed by the story and a T-shirt the teenager offered as proof, Mary Jo Buttafuoco decided that the conversation was over and turned away. As she stepped back into the house, she suddenly fell with a bullet at the base of her skull.

The following year would be enlivened by an antic cavalcade of lawyers, tabloid reporters, Hollywood film makers and the participants themselves—all openly playing with the truth about why Mary Jo Buttafuoco was shot. Conflicting stories became a profitable commodity to be bought and sold in the form of newspapers, magazines, tell-all books, and television shows. By the time the justice system was finished with the affair, Americans would be fascinated or repelled by a story in which nearly all of the action took place out of the courtroom.

When Mary Jo Buttafuoco began to write a description of her assailant for the detectives clustered around her hospital bed, her husband, Joey, suddenly announced that he knew the identity of the attacker. He steered police toward the teenaged daughter of one his customers.

Police quickly arrested 17-year-old Amy Fisher, who claimed that she had been having a sexual affair with Joey Buttafuoco since she was 16 years old. She said she was obsessed with the auto-body mechanic and had gone to the Buttafuoco home to confront his wife. When Buttafuoco's wife refused to take her seriously, Fisher angrily smacked Mary Jo in the head with a cheap handgun, causing it to accidentally discharge and fall apart.

Anyone who assumed that Fisher was merely a smitten teenager confused by the promises of an older lover got a rude shock a week after the shooting. In a secretly made videotape pur-chased by the tabloid television program *A Current Affair,* Fisher was seen negotiating terms for sex with a salesman in a motel bed-room. The videotape aired on national television the night before her bail hearing. What had been a sordid local story became an instant national sensation.

Calling her a prostitute who had stalked Mary Jo Buttafuoco for months, Nassau County Assistant District Attorney Fred Klein charged Fisher with attempted second-degree murder, first-degree assault, and a host of firearms-related felonies. Klein asked for a record-breaking $2-million bail.

If Fisher were a call girl, replied her attorney, Eric Naiburg, then Joey Buttafuoco was a pimp who had introduced his client to prostitution by setting her up with work at an escort service. Nassau County Supreme Court Justice Marvin Goodman was not convinced by Naiburg's arguments that Fisher was a victim of Buttafuoco's manipulations. The judge agreed to the prosecutor's unprecedented $2-million bail request and sent Fisher off to jail to await trial.

LONG ISLAND LOLITA

The media latched onto the tale of the "Long Island Lolita" with an obsession that rivaled Fisher's hunger for Buttafuoco's affection. Reporters looking for a fresh angle in the case were rewarded within days. While tending to his recovering wife at home, Joey Buttafuoco dialed controversial talk radio personality Howard Stern to denounce the sensational stories about his involve-ment with Fisher. Over the airwaves, Buttafuoco announced to the

Joey Buttafuoco escorts his wife, Mary Jo, into the courthouse in Mineola, New York, on May 4, 1993. He was charged with the statutory rape of Amy Fisher, the Long Island teenager who shot Buttafuoco's wife in September 1992.

world that he loved his wife and was innocent of any part in her shooting. He declared that Fisher's claims were hallucinations.

Television and press reporters swarmed around Joey Buttafuoco. Was it true that Long Island escort services called him "Joey Coco-Pops" because of his ability to procure cocaine and women for customers? Buttafuoco admitted that he once had a drug problem, but said that it was now behind him. Had he met Fisher for sex at motels, his boat, his auto body shop, and at her parents' house, as she claimed? Had he encouraged her to kill his wife? Absolutely not, repeated Buttafuoco, who blandly insisted that such charges were the lies of a sick young woman. Buttafuoco said that he only knew the teenager from his auto body shop where she had brought her smashed car for repairs. She was such a frequent customer that he had her telephone beeper number.

As Mary Jo Buttafuoco regained her speech, she vigorously defended her husband. "The story is pretty simple," she told the press. "I love my Joey. My Joey loves me." If she suspected her husband of being involved in the shooting, she said, she would castrate him. "I'm no pushover who doesn't know her ass from her elbow," she told the *Ladies Home Journal.*

HOLLYWOOD DEALS

With Judge Goodman repeatedly refusing to lower Fisher's huge bail, her attorney went to Hollywood to obtain bail money. Naiburg constructed a deal in which a film production agency secured the rights to Fisher's story by guaranteeing the major portion of her bail. The contract was signed and Fisher was released.

When prosecutors learned that Hollywood had helped finance Fisher's bail bond, they were furious. Since 1977, New York's so-called "Son of Sam" law, named after serial killer David Berkowitz, had barred criminals and defendants under indictment from selling their stories for profit. Six months before Fisher's case, however, the law had been declared an unconstitutional infringement of First Amendment rights to free speech. The state was hurriedly modifying the voided law in a way that would comply with the U.S. Supreme Court's decision, while still making convicts liable to financial claims by their victims. The prosecution charged the defense with improperly funding Fisher's release. However, Fisher remained free, Although under a restraining order to stay away from the Buttafuocos. This was not enough for an angry Mary Jo Buttafuoco, who filed a civil suit against Fisher for over $100 million, including the Hollywood bail money.

Meanwhile, the Buttafuocos were also selling interviews and cutting deals with Hollywood. Partially paralyzed and suffering from impaired vision and hearing, Mary Jo Buttafuoco sold the rights to her side of the story to CBS television for several hundred thousand dollars.

On September 23, 1992, Amy Fisher agreed to plead guilty to the lesser charge of reckless assault rather than face the uncertain outcome of a trial for attempted murder. Mary Jo Buttafuoco was livid over the plea bargaining, which required Fisher to aid investigators still examining the incident. This was a clear indication that Joey Buttafuoco was vulnerable to a statutory rape charge if it could be proved that he had had sex with Fisher when she was 16 years old.

"She tried to kill me and now she's taking my husband and trying to destroy us," said Mary Jo Buttafuoco. "This girl is an attempted murderer, a liar, a prostitute, and the D.A. is accepting her statement that she and Joe were together. Something's wrong here."

Free on bail while awaiting sentencing, Fisher visited a boyfriend, Paul Makely. While she rattled on about marrying Makely so that she could have conjugal visits in prison and about a sports car she hoped her notoriety could buy her, Makely secretly videotaped the conversation. He sold the tape to *Hard Copy,* a national tabloid television show, and Fisher made headlines again. When she saw the tape, she attempted suicide and checked into a psychiatric hospital. After she was released, she voluntarily returned to prison to avoid the media.

"I prostituted myself, lied to my parents and friends, shot a woman and gave up what could have been some of the best years of my life—all in the name of 'love' . . . Don't let this happen to you," Amy Fisher, writing in *MOUTH2MOUTH.*

By now, police investigators had collected a handful of motel receipts signed by Joey Buttafuoco on dates when Fisher claimed to have met with him. F.B.I. handwriting analysts confirmed that most of the receipts carried Buttafuoco's signature. Yet facing a lack of any other evidence and with Fisher's reputation making her a useless witness, the District Attorney announced that Buttafuoco would not be indicted.

At her sentencing on December 1, 1992, Fisher listened as Mary Jo Buttafuoco told the court of the lifelong pain she would endure as a result of her gunshot wound and the permanent disruption of her life and those of her loved ones.

"A WALKING STICK OF DYNAMITE"

When her turn to speak came, Fisher nervously apologized, but continued to insist that Joey Buttafuoco had encouraged her.

Judge Goodman was unmoved. "You are a disgrace to yourself, your family, and your friends," he told Fisher as he imposed the maximum sentence of 5-to-15 years imprisonment. "You were like a walking stick of dynamite with the fuse lit."

Eighteen-year-old Amy Fisher listens intently at the beginning of a court hearing on July 29, 1992, during which she was ordered to stay away from Mary Jo Buttafuoco, her husband Joey and their family. The Long Island teen appeared in court again, on September 24, 1992, pleading guilty to assault charges. Fisher shot Mary Jo Buttafuoco, her lover's wife, in September 1992. AP/Wide World Photos

The Buttafuocos happily declared they were satisfied with the verdict and used the occasion to once again brand Fisher a liar.

Major television networks soon aired the made-for-TV movies whose broadcast rights had floated Fisher's bond and paid the Buttafuocos's medical and legal bills. Local interest in the crime had faded. Ratings for the movies, however, demonstrated that viewers around the nation still had not tired of watching the cheap plot play out.

JOEY'S TROUBLES ARE NOT OVER

With Fisher in prison and the television dr.
soon started anew for Joey Buttafuoco. Police qu
employee of his body shop who claimed to have .
boast of having sex with Fisher. On April 15, 199
after his wife was shot, Buttafuoco was indicted o.
statutory rape, twelve counts of sodomy, and one coun
ing the welfare of a child. Buttafuoco pled not guilty a
in a white Cadillac accompanied by his still supportive w

That summer, Mary Jo Buttafuoco accepted an undisclosed settlement in her $125-million damage suit against Fisher and Peter
Guagenti, who was spending six months in prison for selling Fisher
the handgun and driving her to
the Buttafuoco house. The New
York State Supreme Court, however, denied Buttafuoco's claim
to any of the money with which
Fisher made bail, ruling that the
deal with Hollywood was within
Fisher's rights as a presumed
innocent defendant who was permitted to raise bail by any lawful
means.

Domino's Pizza reported that
orders rose 11 percent when Amy
Fisher or either of the Buttafuocos
appeared on the tabloid TV show *A
Current Affair.* —*Wall Street Journal,*
December 7, 1993

The Buttafuocos's frequent press conferences and interviews
on television programs like *The Phil Donahue Show* were viewed by
millions, although the couple's version of events wore thin with
much of the American public. Joey Buttafuoco's constant claims that
he had never slept with Amy Fisher and Mary Jo's feisty denials of
her husband's alleged affair provided easy laughs for comedians
across the nation. Prosecutors were less jocular about the case. They
ordered Buttafuoco to submit to a blood test and physical examination to weigh Fisher's charge that he had given her herpes and her
claim to be able to identify hidden birthmarks on his body.

Joey Buttafuoco's wife stayed home with their children when
he went to court on October 5, 1993. Flanked by his lawyer, Buttafuoco pled guilty to one count of statutory rape, the most serious
charge in a 19-count indictment against him.

"I cannot accept your plea unless you are, in fact, guilty,"
Judge Jack Mackston told the tense defendant. There was a long
pause.

July 2, 1991, I had sexual relations with Amy Fisher at Freeport Motel," Buttafuoco finally said.

"Do you mean sexual intercourse?" interjected the prosecutor.

"Yes, sir."

The defense attorney had an explanation for skeptics, to whom the crumbling of Buttafuoco's claim of innocence was no surprise. "There is a family involved here," Attorney Dominic Barbera said of his client. "That's the man he is. He did what he had to do in that courtroom so everybody else's life could go on."

Those wondering if Buttafuoco had committed a noble perjury to save his family more pain looked to the District Attorney's office, who assured Judge Mackston that factual evidence included motel receipts and witnesses to Buttafuoco's boasts about his sexual relationship with Fisher.

Joey Buttafuoco was sentenced to six months in prison and five years probation. He was also fined $5,000. He left prison after serving only 129 days of the sentence, flashing a thumbs-up sign at photographers. His wife threw a welcome-home party for him and several hundred guests attended. Bemoaning the sensationalism surrounding the case, *The New York Times* printed the party menu and photographed the Buttafuocos celebrating together.

Amy Fisher served her sentence amid tabloid rumors of a romance with a prison guard and later a lesbian affair with a fellow inmate. Meanwhile New York Governor George Pataki eliminated work release for any inmate convicted of a violent felony, thus scuttling Fisher's chance for an early parole.

Joey Buttafuoco considered embarking on a career as an actor, a line of work for which his detractors considered him well-qualified. But Joey's troubles were not over: On May 24, 1995, in Los Angeles, California, he was arrested for—and later pleaded no contest to—soliciting sex from an undercover vice officer. In addition to ordering Buttafuoco to pay $1,715 in fines and take an HIV test, the judge placed Buttafuoco on two years' probation.

Back in Nassau County, Judge Mackston found Buttafuoco guilty of violating his parole and sentenced him to 10 months in prison.

—Tom Smith

I n 1990, an Iowa woman named Cara Clausen found out that she was pregnant. Single and 29 years old, Cara had recently split with her boyfriend, Dan Schmidt, and was dating a man named Scott Seefeldt. Before the birth, she told friends she couldn't care for the baby on her own and would give it up for adoption. When the child was born on February 8, 1991, she named Scott as the father, and within two days, she and Scott signed papers waiving their parental rights.

In Ann Arbor, Michigan, Jan De-Boer, 37, and his wife, Roberta (known as Robby), 32, were eager to adopt. She had had a hysterectomy some years before, so she could not become pregnant. The DeBoers had spent several years sweating out adoption procedures in Michigan, where adoption was legal only through bureaucratic public services. Iowa permitted legal private adoptions. A Cedar Rapids lawyer who was married to Robby DeBoer's cousin, heard about Cara's pregnancy and her plan to give the baby up for adoption. He put the DeBoers in touch with Cara. Another lawyer, John Monroe, took care of the required paperwork, and on March 2, 1991, the DeBoers took the six-day-old baby home, named her Jessica, and looked forward to becoming full legal custodians in six months.

Almost immediately Cara began to have second thoughts. When her old boyfriend Dan showed up, she told him the baby she had just given up for adoption was his, not Scott's. Cara also

Robby and Jan DeBoer with adopted daughter, Jessica, at their home in Ann Arbor, Michigan, just after the July 30, 1993, ruling of the U.S. Supreme Court upholding a lower court order to remove Jessica from their custody. Three days later, the child was returned to her biological parents, Cara and Dan Schmidt, of Cedar Rapids, Iowa. Courtesy Robby and Jan DeBoer; photo by Joni Strickfaden

attended a support-group meeting of the Concerned United Birth parents. There she listened to the sad tales of mothers who regretted giving up their babies for adoption. Before Jessica was more than a month old, Cara and Dan, who were now living together, filed motions to get her back.

It took six months to process genetic tests to prove that Dan indeed was the father. By the end of 1991, an Iowa court, accepting the proof of Dan Schmidt's parenthood and recognizing that he had never signed away his rights, nullified the adoption before it became final. The court ordered the DeBoers to return Jessica to her biological parents, Clara Clausen and Dan Schmidt.

Devastated, the DeBoers decided to fight to keep Jessica. They wrote countless letters to children's rights groups around the country. They contacted reporters. They uncovered the fact that Dan Schmidt had fathered two other children, neither of whom he supported, by two other women, neither of whom he had married.

In January 1992, the Iowa Supreme Court agreed to hear the case, which dragged on throughout the year. Meanwhile, Cara and Dan were married in April 1992. Finally, in December, in an 8-to-1 decision, the higher court upheld the lower court's ruling. Although Dan's fitness as a parent was questionable, it said, his rights held priority over Jessica's. The child was ordered transferred to Iowa immediately.

The DeBoers stood their ground. Despite the Iowa court's finding them in contempt for defying its ruling, they appeared before Judge William Ager, Jr., of Washtenaw County Circuit Court in Michigan. Their lawyer, Suellyn Scarnecchia, argued that Michigan had jurisdiction in the case because Jessica had resided there for at least six months and because the majority of her records and personal relationships were in that state. The judge agreed to assume jurisdiction on behalf of the state of Michigan in order to determine what would be in Jessica's best interest.

On February 12, 1993, citing the testimony of child psychologists that Jessica would bear permanent emotional damage if she were removed from the only parents she had ever known, Judge Ager awarded custody of the child to the DeBoers. Agreeing with their lawyers that there was "much to lose and little to gain" in moving the two-year-old, and turning to the Schmidts, he said, "Think possibly of saying, 'Enough.'" He urged the two couples to keep in touch, but cautioned them not to lead Jessica to believe she had four parents.

Arguing that the judge had acted improperly by assuming jurisdiction from another state, the Schmidts headed for the Michigan Court of Appeals. Within six weeks, in a 3-to-0 decision that ruled only on the question of jurisdiction, that court agreed with the Iowa courts. The DeBoers had 21 days to file an appeal to the Michigan Supreme Court.

Meantime, "Baby Jessica" had become a household name and the case caused millions to more closely consider the risks and

problems of adoption. In about half of all adoptions, the natural fathers, even if they are known, cannot be located. But what if they turn up demanding their "parental rights?" Who knows—wondered columnists, Op-Ed writers, and talk-show hosts—how permanent any adoption is?

Michigan's seven Supreme Court judges heard the arguments. Representing Baby Jessica, Attorney Scott Bassett said the Schmidts were strangers to the child. "These children don't care about biology," he contended. "They know who loves them and who they love." Schmidt lawyer Marian Faupel insisted that the DeBoers had manipulated delays and appeals in order to buy time to bond with the child—to whom they had no legal right. She added that it was not too late for Jessica to bond with her biological parents, for children are not fragile. "They are somewhere between forged steel," she said, "and delicate teacups."

In June 1993, Cara Schmidt gave birth to a second child, Chloe. On July 2, 1993, Michigan's highest court ruled 6 to 1, that Michigan held no jurisdiction in the case over Baby Jessica and that she was to be handed over to the Schmidts within one month.

Jan and Robby DeBoer filed a request for the Michigan Supreme Court to stay its ruling until the U.S. Supreme Court could rule on their request to have the case heard there. The court refused the stay, 6 to 1. Ad hoc "Justice for Jessi" groups began planning bus trips to Washington, D.C., to demonstrate on the steps of the Supreme Court building.

U.S. Supreme Court Justice John Paul Stevens, who handled emergency cases from Michigan for the Court, considered the DeBoers's request to block the order, giving Jessica to the Schmidts. He refused. Their argument, he said, "rests, in part, on the relationship that they have been able to develop with the child after it became clear that they were not entitled to adopt her."

On July 30, 1993, the U.S. Supreme Court refused to lift the deadline for Jessica's return to her natural parents. Justices Harry A. Blackmun and Sandra Day O'Connor dissented. "This is a case that touches the raw nerves of life's relationships," wrote Justice Black-

Suellyn Scarnecchia, attorney for Jan and Robby DeBoer, takes Baby Jessica from the DeBoers's Ann Arbor, Michigan, home on August 2, 1993. Assisting her are two security guards, Norm Nickin (ctr) and John Israel (l). Jessica was being transferred from her adoptive parents, the DeBoers, to her biological parents, Dan and Cara Schmidt in Iowa.

mun. "I am not willing to wash my hands of this case at this stage, with the personal vulnerability of the child so much at risk."

Three days later, the 2½-year-old was carried, screaming, from the DeBoers's home by their lawyer, Suellyn Scarnecchia, and placed in the back seat of a minivan filled with Jessica's favorite toys, clothing and bedding. With Cara and Dan Schmidt, Jessica flew the 400 miles from Ypsilanti, Michigan, to Cedar Rapids, Iowa, by private plane. She napped during half the trip, then awoke and played contentedly with her toys. When they landed, Baby Jessica had a new name, Anna Jacqueline Schmidt.

Nine months later, Jan and Robby DeBoer successfully adopted a newborn boy. His name is Casey.

Before Baby Jessica had met her natural father Dan Schmidt, she met both her grandmothers when they paid a surprise visit to the DeBoers's Ann Arbor home in June 1993. Roberta later recalled them as nice and had told Jessica to call each of them Grandma. But upon leaving, Cara Schmidt's mother advised Roberta, who had been caring for the child for 2½ years, to "take good care of our baby." —*Time*, July 19, 1993

Meanwhile, child psychoanalyst Lucy Biven, who supervised Baby Jessica's transition to the Schmidt home, where she is now known as Anna Lee, reported that "her adjustment has been so unexpectedly good that I give the Schmidts and the DeBoers a lot of credit." And, a year after the transfer, Cara Schmidt said, "Everyone guaranteed—*guaranteed*—that she would have short-term trauma, that she wouldn't eat, wouldn't sleep, she'd cry. It didn't happen. She progressed rapidly."

—Bernard Ryan, Jr.

In June 1989, 53-year-old Janet Adkins of Portland, Oregon, was diagnosed with Alzheimer's disease—the nation's fourth-leading cause of death, which manifests itself as the irreversible deterioration of brain cells. A Renaissance woman, Janet had taught English and piano, taken up hang gliding when her three sons were grown, traversed the mountains of Nepal, and climbed Oregon's highest peak, Mount Hood. Determined not to put herself or her family through the agony of Alzheimer's, she began to plan her own death.

When Adkins heard about Dr. Jack Kevorkian, a 62-year-old pathologist in Royal Oak, Michigan, who had invented a suicide device, she got in touch with him.

Dr. Kevorkian was known among medics as an eccentric. Officials had forced him out of his residency at the University of Michigan Hospital in 1958 when he proposed medical experiments on death-row prisoners. Since 1982, his ideas on euthanasia had prevented his getting an appointment in a hospital. But, he was still licensed to practice medicine in Michigan and California.

Over several weeks, Kevorkian talked frequently with Janet. He ascertained that her determination to kill herself was clear. But, in Oregon, causing or assisting a suicide was a felony. Michigan had no such statute.

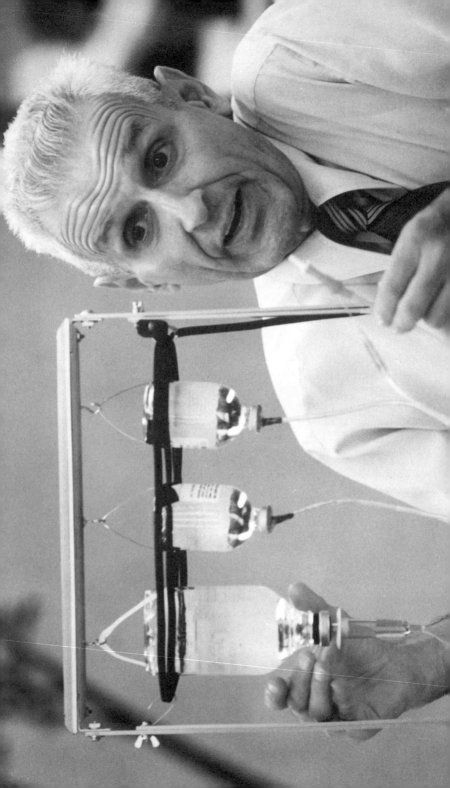

In June 1990, Janet Adkins and her husband flew to Michigan. Over dinner, Kevorkian explained the suicide procedure. Over the next two days he tried to find a motel, funeral home, or vacant office to permit Janet Adkins's suicide on its premises. He explained that he had to tell them what he was doing so they wouldn't sue him later for emotional distress. All efforts failed. Finally, he drove Janet in his own rusty 1968 Volkswagen van to a campsite that had electrical hookups. He attached an electrocardiogram to monitor Janet's heart; next he inserted an intravenous needle into her arm to drip harmless saline solution. Then, as Adkins pressed a button on the machine, stopping the saline and starting the thiopental, which induced unconsciousness, she said, "Thank you, thank you, thank you." A minute later, the machine switched to potassium chloride, which stopped Adkins's heart. The doctor called 911 and, when the police came, told them what he had done. Within hours, his name was being heard in households across America.

THE PUBLIC DEBATE OVER ASSISTED SUICIDE BEGINS

Four days later, a New York Times/CBS News Poll found 53 percent of Americans said a doctor should be allowed to assist an ill person in taking his or her own life. But Judge Alice Gilbert of Michigan's Oakland County Circuit Court ordered Kevorkian to stop using his machine. Talk shows, newspaper and magazine editorials and Op-Ed pages, nursing homes, medical and legal societies all vibrated with the debate over the ethical issue. "I'm trying to knock the medical profession into accepting its responsibilities," explained Kevorkian, "and those responsibilities include assisting their patients with death."

In December, Oakland County prosecuting attorney Richard Thompson charged Kevorkian with first-degree murder. But, Oakland County District Court Judge Gerald McNally found no probable cause that the doctor had committed murder, because Michigan had no law against assisting suicide.

The prosecutor asked the court to forbid Kevorkian to regain possession of his "death machine" from the police, build another like it, or help anyone else build one. Defense lawyer Geoffrey Feiger argued that, since the doctor had been cleared of criminal

Dr. Jack Kevorkian displays a most controversial instrument, his suicide machine, in Detroit, Michigan, on October 25, 1989. Kevorkian helped many terminally ill patients commit suicide with his homemade intravenous device.

charges, the prosecution had no legal basis for its request. On February 5, 1991, Judge Gilbert ruled that Dr. Kevorkian could no longer use the machine.

Two days later, on February 7, the doctor told reporters he intended to use the machine again. In October 1991, in a remote cabin outside Pontiac, Michigan, he helped two women kill themselves. One, who had multiple sclerosis, used a somewhat different intravenous device. Instead of pushing a button, as Janet Adkins had done, the MS victim had two strings attached to her fingers. She pulled the first to activate the anesthetic. Then, as she lost consciousness, her falling arm pulled the second string to start sending sodium Pentothal, a poison, into her system. The other woman, who suffered from a pelvic disease, breathed carbon monoxide, a poisonous gas. Upon hearing of the deaths, Judge McNally commented to an AP reporter, "There is a place for this in society. You can't put this in dark alleys or cabins."

MICHIGAN SUSPENDS KEVORKIAN'S LICENSE

Within a month the eight-member Michigan Board of Medicine suspended Kevorkian's license indefinitely. The suspension, they hoped, would make it impossible for him to get or prescribe lethal drugs and, if he again assisted a suicide, would expose him to the criminal charge of practicing without a license.

Dr. L. J. Dragovic, the Oakland County medical examiner, ruled that both women's deaths were homicides because "suicide is reserved for self-inflicted death" and "all the evidence indicates these deaths were brought about by another person."

In February 1992, the doctor was indicted on two counts of murder and one of delivery of a controlled substance. Free on $15,000 bond, Kevorkian advised a California dentist by telephone and mail on how to kill himself with a suicide machine. The dentist did in fact proceed with his suicide.

On May 15 in Clawson, Michigan, Dr. Kevorkian provided the canister of carbon monoxide as another multiple sclerosis victim killed herself. Again the medical examiner ruled homicide. On July 21, Michigan Circuit Court Judge David Breck dismissed the earlier murder charges, saying the doctor had merely assisted the suicides, which was not illegal in Michigan.

September and November, 1992, brought two more Kevorkian-assisted suicides. This prompted Michigan's House of Representatives to vote, 72 to 29, to ban assisted suicide for 15 months while a state commission studied the issue. "It's a bill against one person," said the doctor. "It's like we're still in the Dark Ages."

The ban was to begin March 30, 1993. In January and February, Dr. Kevorkian helped eight more terminally ill patients commit suicide. Each time, the police confiscated the doctor's paraphernalia. And each time he built a new machine. Incensed, the Legislature passed a hurry-up ban for Michigan Governor John Engler to sign on February 25.

THE SEVERELY ILL ASK KEVORKIAN FOR HELP

The public debate grew intense. California suspended Kevorkian's license. From all over America, the hopelessly ill and severely pained called day and night begging the doctor to help them. In May 1993, he was arrested, then released in his lawyer's custody, for merely being present at a suicide.

Then Michigan Circuit Court Judge Cynthia Stephens declared the hurry-up 15-month ban unconstitutional because it was passed without public hearings and contained more than one objective.

Helping his seventeenth suicide, Kevorkian dared the authorities to prosecute him under the questionable law, which was under review by the Michigan Court of Appeals. On August 17, 1993, he was indicted. "I welcome going on trial," he said. "It isn't Kevorkian on trial. It isn't assisted suicide on trial. You know what's on trial? It's your civilization and society."

Euthanasia a hot topic: In 1991, Derek Humphrey's controversial guide to suicide spent 18 weeks on the bestsellers list—*Final Exit* was the eighth longest-running work of nonfiction on the list that year.

—*Publishers Weekly*, January 1, 1992

Eight hours after the judge ordered him to stand trial, the doctor helped his eighteenth suicide. Some one hundred Friends of Dr. Kevorkian rallied before his apartment building. Neighbors expressed fond support when the doctor said that, if jailed, he would go on a hunger strike.

In October, the doctor assisted his nineteenth suicide—the first in his own apartment in Royal Oak, Michigan. Arrested and refusing to post bail or walk from the courtroom, he was dragged to jail. After Jack DeMoss, a stranger who opposed assisted suicide, bailed him out, the doctor helped his twentieth suicide.

COURTS GRAPPLE WITH THE ISSUE

December 1993 saw Dr. Kevorkian returned to jail on his third charge of breaking the 15-month ban. He refused to post bond or consume anything but fruit juice, water, and vitamins. After ten days, unshaven, weak and gaunt, he was pushed into the courtroom in a wheelchair for a hearing. Three days later, Wayne County Chief Judge Richard C. Kaufman declared the controversial law unconstitutional. In barring all assisted suicide, he said, the Michigan legislature had passed a statute that was too broad to be consistent with rights guaranteed by the U.S. Constitution. The judge cited a 1990 U.S. Supreme Court ruling that affirmed the right to refuse life-supporting medical treatment and found that "when quality of life is significantly impaired by a medical condition and the medical condition is unlikely to improve" the person has a "constitutional right" to commit suicide. Oakland County Prosecutor Thompson, holding the doctor in jail, said the ruling was not binding in his jurisdiction.

Then, later in December and after nearly three weeks in jail, Dr. Kevorkian promised to stop helping suicides "until we get some resolution of this from the courts." A jury trial in the spring of 1994 found him not guilty of violating the ban on assisted suicide even though he admitted to helping a suicide in 1993. Next, the Michigan Court of Appeals reinstated the two murder charges from 1991. The doctor appealed that ruling to the state Supreme Court. Meanwhile, the Court of Appeals found the 15-month temporary ban unconstitutional for technical reasons. Prosecutor Richard Thompson appealed.

Hours after the 15-month ban ended, in his first assisted suicide in more than a year but his twenty-first altogether, Dr. Kevorkian helped a Royal Oak, Michigan, woman commit suicide in her home. She had had both legs and one eye removed because of rheumatoid arthritis and advanced osteoporosis. Two weeks later, the Michigan House of Representatives, in a lame-duck session, rushed through a new bill to take effect April 1, 1995, outlawing assisted suicide. It then moved in an apparent contradiction, for a state-wide voter referendum in November 1996. The state's Senate passed a similar bill but did not call for a referendum. At the same time, the Michigan Supreme Court reversed the Court of Appeals decision and said the Legislature had acted within the constitution in banning doctor-assisted suicides. By this time, the 15-month ban had already expired.

The court also declared that, even without a law, helping a suicide "may be prosecuted as a common-law felony" with a five-year prison term. "This," said Dr. Kevorkian, "is a perfect, clear manifestation of the existence of the inquisition in this state, no different from the medieval one." Attorney Feiger, who had beaten every criminal charge ever brought against the doctor, said "I am ready to take on 21 murder trials, starting tomorrow. No jury will ever convict Dr. Kevorkian. They couldn't even convict him of assisted suicide."

ASSISTED SUICIDE ALSO DEBATED ON WEST COAST

On May 2, 1994, a Michigan jury acquitted Kevorkian of criminal charges in assisting the suicide of Thomas Hyde, a young man suffering from Lou Gehrig's disease. The next day, in Seattle, U.S. District Judge Barbara J. Rothstein ruled in a suit brought by three terminally ill patients, five doctors, and Compassion in Dying—an organization that supports those who seek help to commit suicide. The judge found that a Washington state law that made helping a suicide a felony offense was unconstitutional. Under the 14th amendment to the U.S. Constitution, she decided that adults who are terminally ill and mentally competent have a right to doctor-assisted suicide. An appeal by opponents was still pending in spring 1995.

Election day, November 8, 1994, found Oregon voters in favor of a law permitting doctors to prescribe lethal drugs to terminally ill patients who ask for them. Scheduled to take effect December 8, the law required the patient to ask for the prescription at least twice orally and once in writing, with a lapse of at least 15 days between the first request and the prescription date. The new law was immediately challenged by a coalition of patients, doctors, and other health-care providers. U.S. District Judge Michael Hogan put the law on hold while its constitutional aspects could be reviewed. Hearings were expected to last well into 1995.

Meanwhile in Washington state a federal judge ruled that assisted suicide is a constitutional right. The 9th U.S. Circuit Court of Appeals—the same court that put the Oregon law on hold—overturned the ruling.

On January 14, 1995, in Michigan, Oakland County Prosecutor Tom Ayleworth dropped charges against Dr. Jack Kevorkian for helping Stanley Ball, 82, and Mary Biernat, 73, commit suicide on February 4, 1993. The prosecutor said he lacked sufficient evidence to charge the doctor.

On April 24, the U.S. Supreme Court refused to hear two cases, one of them brought by Kevorkian, which would have brought the question of assisted suicide before the highest court in the nation for consideration.

In May Kevorkian was in the news again. The *Detroit Free Press* reported on May 10 that the body of Rev. John Evans was almost cremated before officials learned his death was an assisted suicide. Because the retired minister had long suffered from lung disease, the death was treated as a natural one until Kevorkian attorney Geoffrey Fieger stated otherwise in a press conference. On May 12, near Pontiac, Michigan, the retired pathologist was present when a 27-year-old man from Phoenix "ended his life mercifully after suffering horribly" from Lou Gehrig's disease. The man, Nicholas John Loving, died in the same 1968 Volkswagen van that Janet Adkins had died in June 1990. Adkins was the first of the now 23 people Dr. Kevorkian had helped take their own lives. Oakland County Prosecutor Richard Thomson commented that "it is very important for people to understand that mere presence in a room where a suicide occurs is not a crime. . . . You have to be able to prove he assisted in some specific way."

The doctor's five-year battle with authorities took a new twist in late-June when he attended his 24th death—this time in his "obitorium" (suicide clinic) in Springfield Township, Michigan. An autopsy into the death of 60-year-old Erika Garcellano, who had suffered from Lou Gehrig's disease for three years, found she died of carbon monoxide poisoning. The death was ruled a homicide. Officials shut down the clinic—a sparsely furnished building that Kevorkian was renting. On August 21, Esther Cohan, a 46-year-old Illinois woman suffering from MS, became Kevorkian's 25th assisted suicide. This death, too, was ruled a homicide.

While public opinion remained divided over the question of assisted suicide, on September 14, Kevorkian was ordered to stand trial for assisting in the 1991 suicides of two Michigan women (trial date set for April 1, 1996) and for two 1993 suicide cases (trial date, February 12, 1996).

—Bernard Ryan, Jr.

In the early hours of March 3, 1991, motorist Rodney King was stopped by Los Angeles, California, police officers after a three-mile, high-speed chase. According to arrest reports filed later, King refused orders to exit the car, then he put up such a struggle that officers were forced to use batons and stun guns to subdue him. However, unbeknownst to police, the entire incident had been captured on video by someone living near the scene of the arrest, and the resulting 81-second tape told a different story. In it King seemed to offer little resistance as several officers kicked and beat him to the ground while a dozen of their colleagues looked on. Public outrage led to a grand jury investigation and indictments against four officers for assault and use of excessive force.

Because of the extraordinary pre-trial publicity, a defense motion to move the proceedings from Los Angeles succeeded, and on March 4, 1992, the trial began in suburban Simi Valley. In his opening speech, Chief Prosecutor Terry L. White referred to falsified reports submitted after the incident as evidence that the police had realized the illegality of their conduct and had tried to conceal it. But it was the evidence of another California Highway Patrol Officer, Melanie Singer, that yielded the most prosecutorial advantage. She testified that defendant Laurence Powell had unnecessarily struck King six times with his metal baton. "He had it in a power swing, and he struck the driver right across the top of the cheekbone, splitting his face from the top of his ear to his chin," she said. "Blood spurted out." Singer did say that defendants Stacey C. Koon and Theodore J. Briseno tried to restrain Powell from beating King further.

King, a tall, heavyset man and former convict, was never called to the stand by the prosecution, a decision reportedly based on the prosecution's fears that he would make a poor impression on jurors.

Under questioning, Briseno admitted that he did not consider King's actions to be threatening, and he repeatedly described co-defendants Laurence M. Powell and Timothy E. Wind as "out of control." He further blamed Sergeant Stacey Koon, the highest ranking officer present, for not intervening.

It was the defense's contention that the officers had believed King to be under the effects of PCP, a powerful hallucinogenic drug, and therefore extremely dangerous. (King had acknowledged that he had been drinking, but there was no evidence that he had taken any drugs.) In his closing statement Defense Attorney Michael P. Stone said of the tape, "We do not see an example of unprovoked police brutality. We see, rather, a controlled application of baton strikes, for the very obvious reason of getting this man into custody."

The jury clearly agreed with this argument. On April 29, 1992, it returned not guilty verdicts for all defendants, deadlocking on only one charge against Powell.

RIOTS RAVAGE LA, THE NATION WATCHES

The April 29 verdict rocked Los Angeles. Within hours the city erupted in rioting that left 58 people dead, more than 2,300 injured, and caused $1 billion in damages. In the aftermath of this tragedy, the U.S. Government filed charges of civil rights violations against the four officers.

Prosecutors Barry F. Kowalski and Steven D. Clymer faced an uphill task when the trial on federal charges began in Los Angeles on February 3, 1993: to convince a jury that the officers had *deliberately* intended to deprive Rodney King of his constitutional rights. The first order of business was to select that jury. The absence of black jurors in the state trial had kindled a firestorm of criticism, but on this occasion a more ethnically diverse panel was selected who heard Clymer make the opening argument. "Rodney King is not on trial," he said. "The issue of whether he is guilty or innocent that night is not the issue in this trial." He added, "What we will tell you is that while he was being beaten while he was on the ground he didn't kick a police officer, he didn't punch a police officer, he didn't grab a police officer, he didn't injure a police officer."

Confirmation of this came from Dorothy Gibson, an eyewitness. "He [King] was lying on the ground, face down with his hands stretched out like a cross shape." Another eyewitness, Robert Hill, described hearing King scream in pain as officers beat him.

Sergeant Mark Conta, an expert on police procedure with the Los Angeles Police Department (LAPD), condemned the tactics used. "It is my opinion that it was a clear violation of Los Angeles police policy." Conta singled out Koon for special criticism. "He should have stopped this and should have taken care of his officers when they needed him most."

Following the first trial it was widely believed that the prosecution had miscalculated by not putting King on the witness stand. On this occasion King did testify and made an effective witness. Describing his actions to Kowalski, he said, "I was just trying to stay alive, sir." King admitted that when the officers began baiting him, chanting, "What's up, nigger? How do you feel, killer?" he had responded defiantly. "I didn't want them to know that what they were doing was getting to me—I didn't want them to get any satisfaction." He described the baton blows as feeling "like you would get up in the middle of the night and jam your toe . . . on a piece of metal. That's what it felt like every time I got hit."

Throughout a grueling day of cross-examination, King did much to dispel earlier defense depictions of him as a menacing brute. Even when Defense Attorney Stone drew an admission from him that he had lied to investigators when he denied driving drunk on the night of the beating, King managed to salvage the situation, saying that, as a parolee, he had been afraid of being returned to prison.

Another defense team member, Harland W. Braun, hammered away at King's varied and contradictory versions of events that night, implying that King had appended the assertions of racial epithets to enhance his civil suit against the City of Los Angeles. "You can become a rich man," said Braun, suggesting that King stood to gain $50 million in the suit.

King did admit to a faulty memory. "Sometimes I forget things that happened, and sometimes I remember things," he said, conceding an uncertainty about whether the taunts leveled at him had actually included the word "nigger." "I'm not sure. I believe I did hear that." In earlier grand jury testimony, King had made no mention of racial slurs.

Braun was incredulous. "As an Afro-American who admittedly was beaten, you would forget that police officers called you nigger? . . . The fact is that you were trying to improve your case or lawsuit and really didn't care about the impact it would have on anyone else!"

The assault was continued by Paul DePasquale, attorney for Wind, who also highlighted King's hazy recollection of events by referring to an interview in which King had erroneously claimed that he was handcuffed throughout the beating. Despite these inconsistencies, King left the stand largely undiminished.

OFFICER'S TESTIMONY A SETBACK FOR THE DEFENSE

In a strange turn of events, Officer Melanie Singer was called this time for the defense, but the content and manner of her testimony yielded a bonanza for the prosecution. Defense attorneys could only stand aghast as she tearfully condemned their clients' conduct. It was a devastating setback.

In his brutality case against the City of Los Angeles, King initially requested $56 million, about one million dollars for every blow he received.

Now, only the defendants could help themselves. Sergeant Koon was the first to take the stand. Insisting that his actions were a textbook example of how to subdue an aggressive suspect, he said, "My intent at that moment was to cripple Rodney King . . . that is a better option than going to deadly force." Koon maintained, King "made all the choices. He made all the wrong choices." In a cool, confident voice, Koon continued, "This is not a boxing match. We had a tactical advantage, and we keep the tactical advantage, and we do not give it up. The tactical advantage is Rodney King is on the ground, and we are going to keep him on the ground."

Laurence Powell (ctr) answers questions from reporters on the steps of the federal courthouse in Los Angeles during his trial. Standing next to Powell is his attorney, Michael Stone, and in the background, Stacy Koon also speaks with several reporters. Powell and Koon were charged with violating the federal civil rights of Rodney King. AP/Wide World Photos

The prosecution was denied an important line of inquiry when Judge John G. Davies barred Clymer from raising allegedly racial passages included in a book written by Koon about the incident. Instead, Clymer could only isolate minor inconsistencies in Koon's testimony. "You are exaggerating, are you not, the amount of things you say happened?"

"No, sir," Koon replied firmly. "I am telling you my recollection."

To the astonishment of those present, it was announced that none of the other defendants would testify. This left only the closing arguments. Following these representations, Judge Davies gave the jury a careful reading of the complex law involved. Then the jury retired.

LOS ANGELES BRACES ITSELF FOR THE VERDICT

With the media, public officials, and ordinary citizens predicting another round of riots if the four officers were acquitted, the tension built in Los Angeles as the jurors deliberated. Police officers were put on 12-hour shifts, and California Governor Pete Wilson mobilized National Guard units. Gun stores did business at breakneck speed as shopkeepers and residents took measures to protect themselves. One week after the jurors began deliberation, on April 17, 1993, they were back. Koon and Powell were emotionless as they heard the guilty verdicts. Briseno and Wind were acquitted. Koon and Powell were each sentenced to 30 months imprisonment on August 4, 1993.

Few jury decisions have so affected everyday life as the verdicts handed down in the two LAPD officer trials. The first prompted violence on an appalling scale, while an entire city held its breath awaiting the second. And yet, almost unmentioned, in all of the turmoil, was the question of possible double jeopardy, and whether the officers should have been retried for essentially the same crime.

"**W**hat they did was not about being a member of any particular race," said Meg Greenfield in *Newsweek*. In the September 13, 1993, article praising Reginald Denny's rescuers for their humanity and morality, Greenfield went on to quote these courageous people who were somewhere else at the time, saw the beating live on TV, and decided to get through the riot-torn area to aid Denny. Among their remarks were "we need to go help him," "it felt like I was getting hurt," and "the reaction was just, go." The principal rescuers were Lei Yuille (a nutritionist), Bobby Green (a truck driver), Terri Barnett (an unemployed data-control clerk), and Titus Murphy (an unemployed aerospace engineer).

As puzzling as the first verdict may have been, many felt that the subsequent federal trial was predicated more on outrage than on the Constitution.

On August 19, 1994, after a well-publicized and well-funded campaign on behalf of the convicted officers, a Federal Appeals Court upheld the convictions against Koon and Powell, and admonished Trial Judge John G. Davies for the leniency of the sentences.

Rodney King's civil action against the city of Los Angeles concluded on April 19, 1994, when he was awarded damages of $3.8 million. His suit for punitive damages was declined by a jury on June 1, 1994.

REGINALD DENNY: IN THE WRONG PLACE AT THE WRONG TIME

In the midst of the violence that engulfed parts of Los Angeles after the first trial, an incident occurred that achieved almost as much notoriety as the King tragedy itself. It began when a white truck driver named Reginald Denny attempted to negotiate the riot-torn intersection of Florence and Normandie avenues and was set upon by a gang of marauding thugs who beat him senseless with a brick. In a bizarre twist, the sickening assault was taped by a TV news crew. At great personal risk four people, all black, came to Denny's assistance They rushed him to the hospital, where doctors diagnosed a fractured skull. Several arrests resulted in two men, Damian Williams, 20, and Henry Watson, 29, being charged with twelve crimes, the most serious of which was attempted murder. Their bail, set at the unusually high figure of $500,000, raised angry concerns about fairness and meant that both men were incarcerated pending trial.

Among the five physicians who worked together to save Reginald Denny's life were two Black doctors—Dr. Madison Richardson, a surgeon who specializes in facial surgery, and Dr. Lawrence Goodwin, an ophthalmologist. According to *Jet* magazine (June 1, 1992), the doctors agreed that Denny didn't want his case to cause racial division.

When that trial began on August 19, 1993, Assistant District Attorney Lawrence Morrison spoke for the nation: "We will never forget the date of April 29, 1992. We saw vicious and horrible crimes broadcast into our living rooms." He portrayed Williams as a kind of malevolent "traffic cop," directing black-driven vehicles through the intersection to safety, and steering all other cars into the hands of the waiting mob.

Edi M. O. Faal, appearing for the defense, took the stance that Williams and Watson were being made "scapegoats" for the riots. Furthermore, he declared them to be the victims of mistaken identity. Defense arguments, built on the theory that the attack on Denny had been a product of "mob psychology," were strongly rebutted by two prosecution expert witnesses, Professor

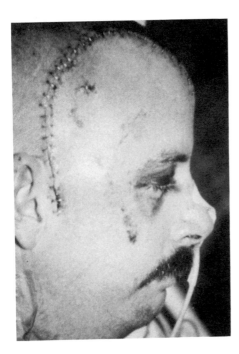

Truck driver Reginald Denny just after his beating in 1992 during the riots that occurred after the acquittal of Los Angeles police officers following the Rodney King trial. The prosecution showed this photo during opening statements on August 19, 1993, when Damian Williams and Henry Watson were charged with beating Reginald Denny. AP/Wide World Photos

Paul Tracy of the University of Dallas and Professor Lawrence Yablonsky of California State University, who described such reasoning as "archaic."

A poignant moment in the proceedings came when Denny, whose recollection of his ordeal was minimal, crossed the court and hugged the mothers of both defendants. Throughout, his dignity and lack of personal rancor helped defuse an otherwise dangerously volatile atmosphere.

On October 1, 1993, the jury, comprised of three blacks, three Hispanics, one Asian, and five whites, retired to reach a verdict. As the days dragged on, it became clear that considerable discord existed behind the locked doors. Finally, on October 11, at the request of the panel, one juror was replaced. The next day a second juror was similarly supplanted. It was a radical step for Judge John Ouderkirk to take, but the majority of jury members made it clear that their complaints had been prompted not by simple intransigence on the part of recalcitrant jurors, but by an almost entire absence of common sense.

After another six days of deliberation, the jury filed back into the courtroom. Doubtlessly aware of the enormous pressure that was being exerted from every direction, they appeared, like their counterparts in the second trial, to opt for something of a compromise. On October 18, 1993, they acquitted both defendants of attempted murder but found Williams guilty of mayhem, for which he received the maximum sentence of ten years imprisonment. Watson, convicted of misdemeanor assault only, was sentenced to four years probation.

Many had feared that this trial would provoke a repetition of the riots 18 months earlier, but Los Angeles took the news calmly.

—Colin Evans

MALICE GREEN CASE

During the evening of November 5, 1992, Malice Wayne Green, a black, unemployed steelworker, stopped his car to drop off a friend at a house in the inner city of Detroit, Michigan. He was observed by two white police officers, Larry Nevers and Walter Budzyn, who were working under cover and who suspected the location was a drug house. They ordered Green to get out of his car. When he refused, they radioed for backup help; then they dragged him out. Noticing that Green kept one fist clenched, the officers ordered him to open it. When he balked, they started beating his fist with their heavy metal flashlights.

While the policemen were beating Green, five additional officers arrived in response to the backup call. By then, it was later alleged, Nevers and Budzyn were hitting Green on the head with their flashlights. One of the five, a white officer named Robert Lessnau, joined in the beating. Another, Sergeant Freddie Douglas, who was the ranking officer at the scene, and who was black, did not participate in the beating; neither did he intervene to stop it.

Malice Green, 34, died that night. The next day, Detroit Police Chief Stanley Knox suspended Nevers, Budzyn, and the five backup officers from the police force without pay. An autopsy a few days later revealed that Green had died of a torn scalp and as many as 12 to 14 blows to the head, and that he had both cocaine and alcohol in his system at the time of his death. On November 16, Wayne County Prosecutor John D. O'Hair charged officers Budzyn and Nevers with second-degree murder. Sergeant Douglas was charged with involuntary manslaughter and willful neglect of duty for failing to stop the beating, and Officer Lessnau was charged with aggravated assault. All four pleaded not guilty. The three other officers were kept on indefinite suspension, but prosecutor O'Hair said he did not have enough evidence to charge them with a crime.

Detroit held its breath. In a city whose population is 75 percent black, most people were probably thinking of the notorious beating of black motorist Rodney G. King by four Los Angeles policemen only the year before and its aftermath: five days of rioting upon the acquittal, in April 1992, of the accused officers on all but one charge. However, Detroit officials were cautious about suggestion an analogy between the King beating, which had been perceived as motivated by racial hatred, and the Green beating. Police Chief Knox said he did not believe that race was a catalyst in this case. Furthermore, when the Detroit officers were charged, the National Director of Special Projects for the National Association for the Advancement of Colored People (NAACP), Jack Gravely, congratulated the police chief and other officials on their prompt reaction by suspending the officers the very next day after the beating. "What is different in Detroit," said Gravely on November 16, "is the leadership. When we compare what happened in Detroit with what happened [in Los Angeles], it does make a difference. Without it, this city probably would still be burning at its walls today."

On December 23, 1992, Michigan District Court Chief Judge Alex J. Allen, Jr., dismissed the charge of involuntary manslaughter against Sergeant Douglas because the beating of Malice Green had already been under way when Douglas arrived on the scene.

The trials of the three remaining police officers raged simultaneously for three months in the Detroit courtroom of Judge Robert W. Crockett III, who was black, and in the homes of America via cable television's Court TV. The evidence was heard by two separate juries. The Nevers jury comprised ten black and two white members. Budzyn's included 11 blacks and one white. Lessnau, facing the lesser charge of assault, found his fate in the hands of Judge Crockett himself rather than a jury.

The prosecution team was led by 36-year-old Kym Worthy, a black lawyer and a graduate of the University of Michigan and the University of Notre Dame Law School, who was already renowned for her skillful use of courtroom dramatics. With her fingernails painted in multiple colors and her long black hair whipping her shoulders as she tossed her head, she had built a solid reputation by winning 90 out of the 100 jury trials she had conducted in nine years with the Wayne County prosecutor's office.

Malice Green was beaten to death by two police officers on November 5, 1992, when they stopped him in his vehicle for a routine inspection. The two Detroit police officers, Larry Nevers and Walter Budzyn, were immediately suspended from duty, and a jury found them guilty of the crime in August 1993. They were sentenced to 12-25 years in prison. *Detroit News*

Officer Nevers testified in his defense that he had been in fear of his life when Malice Green resisted arrest. He admitted that he had hit Green five or six times with his flashlight. Officer Budzyn, on the other hand, denied striking Green and testified that he had not seen officer Nevers or any of the backup policemen club the motorist in the head.

That testimony brought one of the highlights of Prosecutor Worthy's presentation. She pulled a tape measure from her pocket and stretched out two feet of it. "You were this far away from Malice Green and didn't see him being pummeled to death?" she demanded. "You couldn't smell the blood?"

Asked later if such a courtroom stratagem wasn't outside of normal jurisprudence, and if the remark about smelling the blood wasn't inflammatory, Kym Worthy replied, "I don't think it's pushing the lines. I think it's just being thorough. He gave me a story that I didn't think was plausible. I wanted to make sure the jury was able to evaluate it for what it was worth, and I just wanted to show that it wasn't worth too much."

On August 16, Judge Crockett announced that he had reached his decision in the case of Officer Lessnau. August 21 brought the jury's decision in the Budzyn case. Both verdicts, however, were sealed until the end of the Nevers trial. That jury reached agreement on August 23, finding Nevers guilty. Then the Budzyn jury's verdict was also read: guilty. However, the judge found Lessnau not guilty under the charge of assault with intent to cause great bodily harm.

Before they were sentenced, both Nevers and Budzyn apologized to Malice Green's family in the courtroom. Then Judge Crockett pronounced sentence. Larry Nevers, 53, was given 12 to 25 years in prison, with no parole permitted until he served at least nine years and eight months. Walter Budzyn, 47, was sentenced to eight to 18 years, with a minimum of six and a half years. Before they were led from the courtroom, both former police officers asked that they be sent to out-of-state prisons. They said that, as new prisoners, they wanted to dodge any chance of cell block confrontations with prisoners whose incarceration was the result of their work as Detroit policemen. The Michigan Department of Corrections made arrangements for both men to serve their time in Texas. In spring 1995, former officers Budzyn and Nevers were still appealing their cases in Michigan courts.

❞ ... despite the surface similarities with Los Angeles, the police culture in Detroit makes it a very different situation. The department is riddled with problems—but racism hasn't been one of them."

—*Newsweek,* November 20, 1992

—Bernard Ryan, Jr.

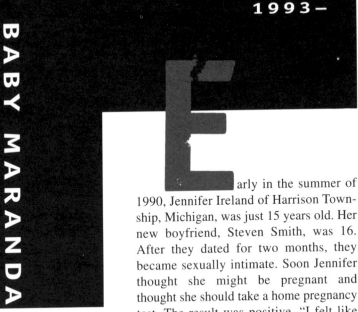

BABY MARANDA CASE

arly in the summer of 1990, Jennifer Ireland of Harrison Township, Michigan, was just 15 years old. Her new boyfriend, Steven Smith, was 16. After they dated for two months, they became sexually intimate. Soon Jennifer thought she might be pregnant and thought she should take a home pregnancy test. The result was positive. "I felt like this was just a dream, and I was going to wake up, and it was all going to go away," she said later. "I was a straight-A student, never did anything wrong. This was not happening to me."

Smith couldn't believe it either. After thinking it over for four days, he told Jennifer he didn't have time for a girlfriend. As a star football player, he had to concentrate on the coming season. They agreed that she would have an abortion.

At an abortion clinic two months later, Jennifer, a Roman Catholic, changed her mind. "I saw all these girls talking about it like it was no big deal," she later admitted, "but I started thinking that I was going to burn in hell for even considering this. So I left."

Although most of Steve Smith's and Jennifer Ireland's schoolmates knew who the father-to-be was, Steve steered clear of Jennifer during her pregnancy. When Maranda Kate Ireland Smith was born on April 22, 1991, he went to the hospital to see her and her now 16-year-old mother, but refused to hold the baby. Putting

Maranda in foster care for three weeks, Jennifer thought about adoption. She decided to raise the child herself. Her mother, a divorced 46-year-old who was a professional nanny, and her 13-year-old sister agreed to help.

Steve Smith was furious. "He said he didn't want her," reported Jennifer, "and I shouldn't want her. He said I was doing the worst thing in the world."

Jennifer had missed two months of her sophomore year in high school. But now, with her mother and sister baby-sitting, she concentrated on her studies and finished in June 1991 with a 3.98 grade point average.

For about a year, Maranda's father stayed away. Then he began to show up to see her more and more often. During this time, he provided no financial support. Finally, Jennifer filed for child support, but none was forthcoming.

In January 1993, Jennifer obtained a court order garnishing $62 a week from Smith's meager income as a high-school student doing odd jobs. However, he managed to have the child support payments cut to $12.

Alleging that Smith grabbed her by the shoulders, shook her, and shoved her into a wall during an argument over visitation rights on Christmas Eve 1992, Jennifer charged Maranda's father with assault. He countersued for custody of the toddler.

"It's a decision made in the 1950s," said Ireland of Judge Cashen's decision. In his statement Cashen said Maranda's paternal grandmother (Debbie Smith) could provide more stability because she is a homemaker.

In June 1993 when Jennifer Ireland graduated from Cardinal Mooney Catholic High School in suburban Detroit, she stood third in her class. The University of Michigan awarded her $11,000 in scholarships as an entering freshman. She packed up Maranda, her toddler toys and clothing, and they headed for the college in Ann Arbor. There, using personal savings, Jennifer Ireland placed her child in a day-care center for 35 hours a week while she attended classes full time. The day-care facility was one recommended by the university.

In March 1994, Steve Smith's countersuit for custody came before Judge Raymond R. Cashen of Macomb County Circuit

Jennifer Ireland poses with her daughter Maranda on July 27, 1994. Jennifer never married the baby's father, Steven Smith, but the couple became involved in a custody battle over the child in 1994. Smith was granted custody of Baby Maranda on June 27, 1994, but the case is under review by the Michigan Court of Appeals. Jack Gruber/*Detroit News*

Court. In the hearing, Smith's lawyer, Sharon-Lee Edwards, attacked Jennifer Ireland's behavior as a mother. Her accusations included drug and alcohol abuse and sexual misconduct. Jennifer denied all such allegations.

Judge Cashen appointed two independent experts to appraise Maranda's situation. The Psychodiagnostic and Family Services Clinic found that Maranda looked to her mother for "guidance, discipline, and the necessities of life" and that she had a strong attachment to both parents. The Macomb County Friends of the Court, a social services agency that performed investigations related to court cases, found nothing to condemn in the environment in which Maranda was being raised. Both organizations recommended that the little girl stay with her mother. The judge himself observed that the three-year-old had lived all her life with her mother, who was her primary care giver, and that such a disruption of family life as a change of custody would be disturbing to her. However, the judge ruled on June 27, 1994, that Maranda should be handed over to her father because her mother had placed her in a licensed day-care facility for 35 hours a week in order to attend college classes. "There is no way," concluded the 69-year-old jurist, "that a single parent attending an academic program at an institution as prestigious as the University of Michigan can do justice to their [sic] studies and the raising of an infant child. A child gains the feeling of security, a safe place, by virtue of permanence." The judge added that he was skeptical about how the child's emotional well-being would be affected by the long-term impact of "strangers."

Child-care experts were astonished. "It was unusual," said Henry Baskin, who, as a state bar commissioner, had helped draft Michigan's child custody act, "for the court to ignore a recommendation from two separate agencies who concluded that the child should be with the mother."

In the same week that Judge Cashen's order was handed down, Smith was arraigned on Jennifer's charge of assault. The domestic violence was "not pertinent" to his decision, remarked Judge Cashen. "The parties in their youthful way apparently crashed or mauled one another," he said. "It is all superfluous." The judge also seemed unimpressed by the fact that Maranda's father had sought custody of her only after her mother pressed the domestic violence charge against him and hauled him into court for child support.

Jennifer Ireland's lawyer, Julie Field, said that 60 different organizations, including the Children's Defense Fund and the Women's Legal Defense Fund, joined in eight amicus briefs supporting Jenny.

—*Good Housekeeping,* February 1995

The household to which the judge consigned Maranda was that of Smith's parents, with whom he was living while attending Macomb Community College and working part-time cutting lawns. His homemaker mother would take care of the child—a provision, said the judge, that was better than having the child "supervised a great part of the time by strangers. Under the future plans of the father, the minor child will be raised and supervised by blood relatives."

The day after he ordered Maranda handed over to her father, Judge Cashen, himself a Roman Catholic who had seven children and 16 grandchildren, told a reporter that "family values" were his "whole background." The written opinion he sent down, he said, was based not on any allegations regarding behavior, but on the fact that the child was put in day care by the mother even though the father's mother was capable of taking care of her.

Within days, the American Civil Liberties Union (ACLU), the National Organization for Women (NOW), the United Auto Workers (UAW), and several other national groups filed a joint friend-of-the court brief on behalf of Jennifer Ireland. *The New York Times* ran a major editorial excoriating Judge Cashen. It concluded:

> Judge Cashen's order . . . stands: an affront and threat to the millions of women for whom day care is the difference between ignorance and an education, poverty and a decent income, dependency and self-reliance. In stigmatizing Jennifer Ireland for her ambition and initiative, Judge Cashen stigmatizes all of them."

After considering the brief, the Michigan Court of Appeals delayed the judge's order. On August 9, 1994, it granted a stay of the transfer of custody of baby Maranda pending review of the case. While the review was expected late in 1994, it was still being awaited in March 1995. Meanwhile, Maranda stayed with her mother.

At a hearing in the Michigan Court of Appeals on May 3, Ireland's attorney, Julie Field of the University of Michigan's Women and the Law Clinic, argued that Judge Cashen's views on day care had tipped the scales in the custody decision. One of the three judges on the panel hearing the appeal, Judge Gribbs said "we do not make decisions for the court below," suggesting that if the appeals court found mistakes, the case would need to be updated before the lower court could rule again on custody. Though the panel was expected to rule in the case within 60 days, as of early October no decision had been handed down.

—Bernard Ryan, Jr.

WOODY ALLEN-MIA FARROW CUSTODY CASE

Woody Allen and Mia Farrow are not Hollywood stars— they stay away from the glamour of tinseltown. They are, nevertheless, famous film people, and millions flock to see their movies. The couple were never married, nor did they live together: During their relationship they inhabited separate apartments on opposite sides of Central Park in New York City. Together they had children and they were a family.

On August 13, 1992, the public gasped when Woody Allen filed suit against Mia Farrow for custody of their three children. Although the three children lived with Farrow, Allen was a frequent household visitor. Moses Amadeus Farrow, 14, a Korean boy, was adopted by Farrow after her divorce from noted symphony director André Previn. Later, the boy was also adopted by Allen. Dylan O'Sullivan Farrow, 7, a girl, was adopted as a baby by Farrow and Allen together in 1985. The couple's natural son, Satchel O'Sullivan Farrow, was 4½ on that fateful day.

While the legal documents in the suit were immediately sealed, an excited public got the details from the celebrities themselves. Two New York newspapers, *The Daily News* and *The New York Post* reported that for the past eight months Allen had been having an affair with Farrow's 21-year-old daughter, Soon-Yi Farrow Previn, a Korean whom the actress had adopted when she was married to Previn. (Altogether, Farrow has 11 children, seven of whom are adopted.) Responding to these reports, Allen put out a press release saying, "It's real and happily all true."

About the same time that Allen filed the custody suit, Connecticut State Police disclosed that they were investigating Allen's alleged sexual abuse of Dylan at Farrow's country home in Bridgewater. The well-known movie maker vehemently denied the allegation. He said it was a weapon used by Farrow to counter his efforts to win custody of the children.

LIFE IMITATING ART?

The battle was joined. Legions of fans were both confused and disappointed. The news media, while proclaiming that all its major sources in the story were the principals themselves, also chased every rumor and interviewed whoever had an opinion. Film buffs wondered how tarnished the reputation of their idol, Allen, would become. Cashing in on the publicity, Allen's studio advanced the opening date of his new movie, *Husbands and Wives,* in which he starred with Farrow and which, according to advance notices, mimicked their real-life breakup and custody battle. The studio announced that the film would be released nationally, rather than in only eight cities, as had previously been scheduled.

At a preliminary hearing, New York Supreme Court Justice Phyllis B. Gangel-Jacob turned down Allen's request for visitation rights with the children. She also refused to accept, from Farrow's lawyers, Allen's photographs of Soon-Yi in the nude—pictures that Farrow had found on the mantel-piece in her home and that had tipped her off that the affair was going on.

By October 1992, the case had become fuel for the raging political fires of the U.S. presidential election year—one of whose themes was family values. U.S. Attorney General William P. Barr, quoting an Allen interview in *Time,* said, "After all, he [Allen] said 'the heart wants what the heart wants.' There you have it. In seven words, Allen epigrammatically captures the essence of contemporary moral philosophy." U.S. Representative Newt Gingrich, known for preaching family values as a Republican strength, told a Georgia audience, "Woody Allen is currently having non-incest with a non-daughter for whom he is a non-father because they have no concept of families . . . it's a weird environment out there."

Next came a wave of hearings and rulings. Acting New York Supreme Court Justice Elliott Wilk ruled that television cameras would be allowed into the court during future hearings and during the trial. Both sides immediately appealed, so Administrative Judge Stanley S. Ostrau barred both TV and radio coverage in his court-room. Meanwhile, Farrow sued in Surrogate's Court to nullify Allen's adoption of Moses and Dylan.

In a December 15, 1992, hearing, Justice Wilk ruled that Farrow must provide Allen a copy of a videotape in which Dylan reportedly said Allen molested her. Wilk also turned down Farrow's request that Allen's suit for sole custody be put on hold pending the outcome of her suit in Surrogate's Court.

On March 18, 1993, a team of psychological investigators at Yale-New Haven Hospital cleared Woody Allen of sexually molesting Dylan. The findings, which were the results of repeated interviews with Allen, Farrow, Dylan, the child's psychologist, and household servants, were not made public. However, Allen's lawyers reported that the videotape on which Farrow had based the accusation was a result either of the child's imagination or of someone else's manipulation.

THE CUSTODY TRIAL BEGINS

The next day, on March 19, 1993, the custody trial began before Acting Justice Wilk. Allen testified that after Farrow learned of his affair with Soon-Yi, she cut his head out of family pictures and that "she [Farrow] called me dozens of times a night, raging and screaming, threatening to kill me." He testified further that he once found a note she left by an open window saying, "I've jumped out the window because of what you've done to the children."

The nude photos of Soon-Yi were admitted as evidence in court. Farrow's attorney, Eleanor B. Alter, suggested they were pornographic. Allen testified they were a matter between consenting adults and were intended to be erotic. Attorney Alter read a letter from Moses Farrow, 15, to Allen that said, "You have done a horrible, unforgivable, ugly, stupid thing. I hope you get so humiliated you commit suicide. . . . Everyone knows not to have an affair with your son's sister, including that sister, but you have a special way to get that sister to think that that is O.K." Questioned by Elkan Abramowitz, his own lawyer, Allen responded that Moses

was manipulated by his mother and used the same words and phrases that she had used only days earlier.

Farrow then testified that Dylan told her the preceding summer that her father had sexually molested her. Farrow conceded, however, that the child, in her shyness, would not tell doctors of the abuse and that a medical examination produced no signs of it. She explained that she had videotaped the girl's statement because, "I wanted this documented because it had happened before. . . . He would creep up in the morning and lay beside her bed and wait for her to wake up. I thought it was excessive. I was uncomfortable all along." Farrow added that when Allen came to visit, Dylan screamed, "Hide me! Hide me!" to her brothers and sisters.

Clinical psychologist Dr. Susan Coates, who had treated Satchel and met often with both parents, testified that she had been convinced by Farrow's behavior—including sending Allen a Valentine with skewers through the hearts of her children—that she might harm herself or Allen.

More than two weeks went by in the stuffy, crowded New York City courtroom where the paint was peeling from the walls and ancient chairs creaked constantly. Dr. Coates testified that Allen should be allowed unsupervised visits with Satchel

Accusations fly, lawyers jump into the fray: Allen's attorney, Elkan Abramowitz, cross-examined Farrow's attorney Alan Dershowtiz "with the relish of a starving man happening across a Big Mac."

—*Washington Post,* April 17, 1993

but was less certain about his seeing Dylan. The children's nanny testified that Farrow was not always a good mother and had once slapped an adopted son across the face for not finding a dog leash. Allen's sister testified that Farrow taught the children to hate him. Allen produced a surreptitious recording of a phone call from Farrow's Connecticut housekeeper that disparaged Farrow's abilities as a mother. Allen's lawyer, Abramowitz, accused the Connecticut State Police of aiding Farrow's case by allowing her lawyers to see the Dylan videotape but refusing his request to see it. A baby sitter testified that she saw Allen kneeling before Dylan "in a way that bothered" her. In a three-hour shouting match between Farrow's

Woody Allen and Mia Farrow in happier days—enjoying the Big Apple Circus at Lincoln Center in New York City, on November 14, 1987. Seated with her two adopted children, Farrow had recently announced that she and Woody were expecting a baby of their own.

attorney, Alan M. Dershowitz, and Allen's attorney Abramowitz, Dershowitz denied allegations by Abramowitz that he had asked Allen to pay millions of dollars to get Farrow to call off the molestation charge. Justice Wilk criticized New York investigators for subjecting Dylan to the trauma of a second sex-abuse investigation. A doctor who headed the Connecticut investigation said that Dylan's story had "a rehearsed quality" and that Farrow might have encouraged the child to fabricate because she liked to perform.

On April 17, 1993, about the verbal brawl between lawyers Dershowitz and Abramowitz, Paul Span of the *Washington Post* wrote that Justice Elliot Wilk had "presided with the air of a parent refereeing between two scrapping children." Faye Ellman Photography

On June 7, 1993, Justice Wilk, in a stinging 33-page decision, called Allen a "self-absorbed, untrustworthy and insensitive father. It is clear," he continued, "that the best interests of the children will be served by their continued custody with Ms. Farrow." The judge denied Allen immediate visitation rights with Dylan, ruling that a further review be held after Dylan received psychological therapy. Supervised visits, however, with Satchel would be allowed. The judge also acceded to Moses's request not to be forced to see his father and ordered Allen to pay Farrow's legal fees. Finally, the judge questioned the findings of the Yale-New Haven Hospital investigators, noting that whether or not molestation took place, "Mr. Allen's behavior toward Dylan was grossly inappropriate."

In September 1993, Connecticut State Attorney Frank Maco announced that, while he had "probable cause" to prosecute Allen on charges of sexual molestation of Dylan, he was dropping the case to spare her the trauma of appearing in court. Allen filed complaints asking the state bar counsel to disbar Maco and requesting that the State Criminal Justice Commission discipline Maco for making an accusation without producing an indictment. In October, the New York State Department of Social Services dropped its investigation into the child molestation charge. It concluded "that no credible evidence was found . . . that the child named in this report has been abused or maltreated." In November, the Connecticut Criminal Justice Commission voted unanimously to dismiss Allen's complaint against Maco. It said that after four hours of deliberation it could find no evidence that Prosecutor Maco had violated the canon of ethics for lawyers in his remarks during the September news conference in which he announced that he was dropping the charges against Allen. In January 1994, the Connecticut bar's disciplinary panel criticized Maco's handling of the case and found that he might have prejudiced the celebrities' custody battle, but that he did not violate the state's code of conduct for lawyers.

THE AFTERMATH

Over the following year, Allen continued to date Soon-Yi, dining with her in the exclusive Manhattan restaurant, Elaine's, where he and Farrow had often been seen in earlier days. Farrow no longer visited the restaurant. Meanwhile, Farrow informally renamed two of her children, calling Dylan by the name Eliza. Satchell became Seamus. On October 5, 1994, Allen lost an appeal for relief from the custody ruling that forbade his seeing Dylan (Eliza) and Moses and allowed court-supervised visits only with Satchel (Seamus).

Both Farrow and Allen went on with their film making. In 1994 Farrow starred with Joan Plowright and Natasha Richardson in *Widow's Peak*, which met with some critical acclaim. Meanwhile, Allen released *Bullets Over Broadway*, which went on to be heavily nominated for Academy Awards.

—Bernard Ryan, Jr.

THE MENENDEZ BROTHERS' TRIAL

On the evening of August 20, 1989, with bowls of strawberries and ice cream in their laps, entertainment magnate José Menendez and his wife, Kitty, were watching television in the den of their Beverly Hills mansion. Unexpectedly, their sons Lyle and Eric allegedly burst through the door with 12-gauge shotguns, killing their parents. Bizarre as it may sound, this bloody "fact" would be the least disputed feature of one of the most controversial court battles of the decade.

Detectives weighing the ferocity of the homicides thought the killings had the look of an organized crime hit. José Menendez, a 45-year-old Cuban immigrant and self-made millionaire, had dealings throughout the film and music distribution industry, including a production interest in Sylvester Stallone's "Rambo" movies. It seemed unlikely that anyone would pump 15 shotgun rounds into the Menendez couple unless that person were trying to make a statement.

As time passed, however, the police took a closer look at the Menendez sons, who were heirs to their parents' $14-million fortune. Lyle, 22, and Erik, 19, spent over a half million dollars on new cars, watches, and a restaurant business soon after their parents' funerals. Suspicious evidence began to accumulate.

In March 1990, police, using search warrants, confiscated the records of Dr. L. Jerome Oziel, the psychotherapist who had been treating the brothers. Lyle Menendez was arrested a few days later. Erik, who had spent part of his inheritance on a personal tennis coach, surrendered to Los Angeles police upon his return from a tournament in Israel. Prosecutors charged that the pampered sons had murdered their parents because of an impatient desire to collect their inheritance.

The most incriminating evidence was said to exist in a tape of one of Dr. Oziel's therapy sessions. A legal battle quickly erupted over whether or not the tape could be admitted as evidence. Under California law, such recordings are confidential under the protection of the patient-therapist relationship. Judge James Albracht, however, ruled that the Menendez brothers had threatened Dr. Oziel's life, thus voiding any claim to confidentiality. After two years of grappling over the issue, the state Supreme Court ruled that only a tape of Dr. Oziel dictating his notes from the session would be admissible as evidence.

If convicted of first-degree murder, Erik and Lyle would face death in California's gas chamber. In an unusual arrangement, the brothers were to be tried simultaneously by the same judge but before two separate juries.

A friend and bodyguard both testified that within a week after his parents were killed, Lyle Menendez went on a shopping spree—for a Porsche, a house, a restaurant, and clothes. —*The Los Angeles Times,* July 28, 1993

Throughout the three years before the Menendez brothers were brought to trial, they repeatedly denied shooting their parents. A week before the trial began on July 20, 1993, however, the brothers admitted to the killings. Nevertheless, they pleaded not guilty, claiming that they had acted in self-defense after years of suffering sexual and emotional abuse at the hands of their parents.

"We are not disputing where it happened, how it happened, who did it," Jill Lansing, Lyle's lawyer, said in her opening statement. "What we will prove to you is that it was done out of fear."

Lansing and Leslie Abramson, Erik's attorney, called over 30 relatives, neighbors, teachers and sports coaches to the stand. They all described José Menendez as a success-obsessed tyrant who com-

pletely dominated his sons' lives, publicly humiliating them whenever he felt their conduct was unsatisfactory. Kitty Menendez was described as depressed, prone to hysterical fits and suicidal over her husband's extramarital affairs. While the Menendez brothers were legally adults when they killed their parents, the defense attorneys consistently referred to them as "children."

After a month of hearing testimony of witnesses who remembered José and Kitty as less than model parents, Judge Stanley M. Weisberg had heard enough. "We're not talking about a child custody case," he snapped. Lansing and Abramson were ordered to put their clients on the stand.

José Menendez had been accused of browbeating his sons to attain excellent grades and high tennis scores. However, when Lyle took the witness stand, he painted a profoundly darker picture of his father's demanding nature. He testified that his father had begun showing the boys pornographic videos and telling them about homosexual bonding rituals between soldiers in ancient Greece when he was six and Eric was three years old. The defense produced nude childhood snapshots of Lyle taken by his father. Lyle recalled his father massaging him after sports practices when he was a child. The rubdowns turned into forced oral sex. When he was seven, Lyle said, his father sodomized him.

On July 21, 1993, *The Los Angeles Times* reported that "decorum was not always the order of the day as more than 60 TV and radio reporters, producers, sound technicians and newspaper reporters descended on the Van Nuys courthouse" to cover the Menendez trials, which were expected to be "lurid and sensational."

"I told my mom to tell Dad to leave me alone, that he keeps touching me," Lyle said. "She told me to stop it, that I was exaggerating, and my dad had to punish me when I did things wrong."

Lyle Menendez (l) in a discussion with his brother Erik during a court hearing in Beverly Hills, California, on April 2, 1991. A delay in the preliminary hearing was granted while the state Supreme Court decided if the alleged murder confession to a psychiatrist should be allowed as evidence or remain protected under doctor-patient privilege.

With tears in his eyes, Lyle said the abuse stopped when he was eight, but that his father threatened to kill him if he ever revealed the truth.

In August 1989 Erik confided to his older brother that José had been sexually molesting him for years. Five days before the killings, Lyle confronted his father.

"What I do with my son is none of your business," Lyle recalled his father retorting. "I warn you, don't throw your life away."

Lyle persisted, telling his father that he would expose the abuse if it continued.

According to Lyle, José replied, "We all make choices in life, son. Erik made his. You've made yours." From that moment on, Lyle felt his and his brother's lives were in danger. "I felt he had no choice but that he would kill us, that he would get rid of us in some way because he thought I was going to ruin him."

Kitty became hysterical after the confrontation. She told Erik that if Lyle "had just kept his mouth shut, things might have worked out in this family." The brothers took this as proof that their parents were planning to kill them soon. According to the brothers, things remained tense in the Menendez household for the next few days. When their parents disappeared into the den, the brothers suspected an attack, got their guns, and burst through the door, firing.

Deputy District Attorney Pamela Bozanich declared that the tales of abuse were nonsense. She made Lyle admit that he had lied to detectives and had discreetly removed shotgun shell casings from his car while police combed the gory crime scene.

The brothers claimed they had bought shotguns for protection. Yet Bozanich established that they had deliberately bought the guns out of town with false identification, paying in cash so that the purchase could not be traced. Bozanich scoffed at Lyle's claim that he placed the muzzle of his shotgun against his fatally wounded mother's cheek and fired because he was "afraid" of her.

On November 3, after Lyle's emotional testimony and Bozanich's fierce cross-examination, the drama halted with a fresh dispute over Dr. Oziel's therapy session tape. Playing of the actual tape had been barred by the pre-trial ruling. During the trial, however, defense attorneys had made the defendants' psychological health a crucial issue. Therefore, Judge Weisberg decided, the tape should be heard.

In an effort to portray their case to its best advantage before the juries, both sides immediately began battling over which one would be able to introduce the tape in court. The judge ordered that the tape be turned over to the prosecution, but allowed the defense to introduce it as evidence.

On the tape, Lyle and Erik said nothing to their therapist about sexual or physical abuse at the hands of either of their parents. They said nothing about killing for their inheritance. They confessed to the shootings, but identifying the killers was no longer the central mystery it had been when police seized the tape over three years earlier. Both sides agreed that the fate of the Menendez brothers now hinged on their motive for killing their parents. The tape gave no answers.

The case took an odd turn as soon as the tape ran out. Ms. Judalon Smyth, Dr. Oziel's former lover, had helped to launch the prosecution's case. In 1990, she had given police a sworn affidavit claiming that she had overheard the Menendez brothers talk about committing "the perfect killing" and threatening Dr. Oziel because he knew too much.

"I can't believe you did this," Smyth swore she had heard Lyle tell Erik. "I can't believe you told him. I don't really have a brother now. I could get rid of you for this. I hope you realize what we're going to have to do. We've got to kill him and anyone associated with him."

Smyth's tip helped police make the arrest. Knowledge of the threat against Oziel was what had allowed the prosecution to bypass patient-therapist confidentiality in introducing the tape.

Now, however, Smyth turned defense witness. Her affair with Oziel, who was married during their relationship, was over. She was suing him for rape, assault, and forcing her to take mind-controlling prescription drugs. When she took the stand at the Menendez trial, she disclaimed her previous statements, saying that the psychotherapist had "brainwashed" her into believing what she told police three years ago. Vexed prosecutors accused Smyth of changing her story in order to take revenge on her former lover.

The defense introduced substantial testimony about the nature of psychological abuse in order to support claims of sexual victimization. Experts explained how the brothers' secrecy, along with their simultaneous attachment to and violence toward their parents, was consistent with the symptoms of "battered wife syndrome."

Six months of testimony had passed when closing arguments began on December 8. Prosecutor Bozanich depicted the brothers as "vicious, spoiled brats" who had killed their parents out of greed and then lied repeatedly to cover their tracks. When they were caught, Bozanich continued, the pattern of lies grew into elaborate tales of abuse intended to gain sympathy. Even if the unproved allegations of abuse were true, however, the brothers should not go free.

"We don't execute child molesters in California. Some of you think we should," Bozanich told the jurors. "But the state does not execute child molesters, and these defendants cannot execute them either."

The defense's demonization of José and Kitty Menendez continued into the final arguments. Some legal observers wondered why the prosecution had not pressed the brothers harder to explain why they had killed their allegedly unstable but unthreatening mother.

"It may be hard for you to believe that these parents could have killed their children," Lansing proposed. "But is it so hard to understand that these children believed their parents would kill them?"

Judge Weisberg's final instructions to the twin juries ruled out acquittals. The judge declared that the facts did not support a plea of "perfect self-defense," in which "a reasonable and honest belief that their own lives were in imminent danger" led the brothers to kill.

The jurors had four options. If it was agreed that the brothers had maliciously plotted to kill their parents, a verdict of first-degree murder could warrant the death penalty. Varying sentences could be imposed for convictions of second-degree murder, voluntary manslaughter or involuntary manslaughter. If the brothers were found guilty of "involuntarily" shooting their parents out of a genuine but unreasonable fear, they could be sentenced to a term shorter than the time served since their arrest.

After 16 days of deliberations, Erik's jury told Judge Weisberg that it could not agree on a verdict. Weisberg ordered the jurors to keep talking, but after nearly three weeks of shouting behind closed doors, the jurors gave up. Judge Weisberg declared a mistrial and released the jurors with a warning not to speak to the media. He did not want Lyle's unsequestered jury to be influenced.

However, two weeks later, on January 28, Lyle's jury reported that it was also deadlocked. As weary attorneys on both sides watched, a second mistrial was declared. Los Angeles District Attorney Gil Garcetti immediately announced that the Menendez brothers would face a second trial for first-degree murder, with no possibility of plea bargaining.

Strong disagreements over the sexual abuse claims had scuttled any chance for unanimous verdicts. With both juries stubbornly divided over the brothers' truthfulness, the final votes were scattered over the three most serious verdicts possible, each with its own implicit, differing degree of guilt. Only one of the 24 jurors had voted for the least serious charge of involuntary manslaughter.

Regardless of his intent, Lyle's testimony indicated that he had made most of the decisions regarding the shootings, with his younger brother passively agreeing to participate. Yet Erik's jury had been the most contentious, with an almost even split between men voting for first-degree murder and women voting for voluntary manslaughter. The female jurors complained that sexist bullying and male jurors' homophobic suspicions about Erik's sexuality had prevented a serious resolution of the case.

Defense attorney Abramson's tough, flamboyant defense had kindled tension between her and Judge Weisberg throughout the first trial. She continued her public assault on the prosecution after the verdict. She faulted the judge for his handling of the case and declared that no jury would ever be able to agree on a verdict. To prove her point, she invited the sympathetic women jurors to her home for dinner, a telephone chat with Erik, and an interview session with reporters about the stormy deliberations in the jury room.

While her detractors accused her of being a media hound, others marveled at her unabashed willingness to exploit the media on behalf of her client. Both critics and sympathizers agreed that publicizing her post-trial dinner aimed to influence the jury pool, while illustrating to the state that plea bargaining might be preferable to the time and expense of a second trial in which jurors might be no more likely to agree on a verdict.

Prosecutors were not impressed. They declared that the defense strategy used so successfully in the first trial would be easier to counter now that it was known. Those who had questioned the sincerity of the Menendez brothers' tears on the witness stand doubted that the defendants would be clever enough to convince a second jury of their emotional fragility.

The trials cost the brothers their inheritance; the vast Menendez fortune was now depleted. Public defenders were appointed to represent Lyle. Erik pleaded with the judge for the State of California to pay his legal fees so that he could retain Abramson as his lawyer. The judge refused. After some grumbling about what a sacrifice it would be, Abramson agreed to stay on the case for a reduced fee.

If the Menendez brothers had killed their parents for money, their reward had vanished. In September 1994, the Menendez mansion was sold at auction for $1.3 million. The money was split between creditors and the county, which demanded restitution for the cost of the defendants' lengthy incarceration. Even their notorious celebrity dimmed. Although the trial of Hollywood Madam Heidi Fleiss and the Menendez brothers' second pretrial hearings were held in the Los Angeles County Courthouse, both legal proceedings were largely ignored by the media, whose attentions had moved en masse to the O.J. Simpson murder trial being held in the same building. Coincidentally, Simpson had visited the Menendez family in the days when he was sprinting though airports in Hertz commercials. José Menendez, then a prominent Hertz executive, invited the former football star to dinner so that his sons could meet him. According to *Vanity Fair* (February 1995), Simpson and the Menendez brothers did not meet again until "they were all in the celebrity section of the Los Angeles County Jail, all three charged with double murder."

On April 3 Judge Stanley Weisberg ruled that the brothers would be retried together and in front of a single jury. This was not the only change in the second trial, which got under way on August 23, 1995: Prosecutors were expected to take a tougher approach to the brothers' allegations of child abuse, Judge Weisberg promised to sharply limit the defense case, the proceedings in the Van Nuys Superior Court would not be broadcast live on TV, and the brothers were now older, 27 and 24. However, the arguments from both sides were the same, with prosecutors claiming Lyle and Erik had acted out of greed and hatred and the defense claiming the brothers had lashed out after years of abuse.

—Tom Smith

O f all crimes, sexual molestation charges made by children are among the most troubling and difficult to prove. Public revulsion and fear combine to ensure that allegations of such misconduct usually become widely known, even before a case reaches court. In 1993, when suspicions fell on Michael Jackson, the highest-paid entertainer on earth, the sordid accusation was literally heard around the world.

On August 23, 1993, Los Angeles police announced that international pop star Michael Jackson was the subject of a criminal investigation. Although details were withheld, rumors that a complaint charging the 35-year-old singer with sexually abusing a young boy instantly leaked to the media. Just as quickly, Jackson's lawyer, Bert Fields, and his private detective, Anthony Pellicano, charged that the investigation stemmed from a failed extortion attempt against the pop star. While the singer was performing in Asia, police with search warrants swarmed over Jackson's 2,700-acre Neverland Valley Ranch near Santa Barbara, California.

Three weeks later, the story began to emerge. An unnamed 13-year-old boy who, with his mother, had been a frequent guest at Jackson's estate, had given a statement to a Department of Children's Services psychologist, charging Jackson with repeated acts of sexual abuse. Under California law, the psychologist duly informed police. As an investigation began, the boy and his family filed a civil suit against Jackson, charging him with sexual battery, seduction, willful misconduct, intentional infliction of emotional distress, fraud, and negligence.

Lawyers for both sides postured for public sympathy as the state's criminal investigation for facts proceeded quietly in the background. The unnamed youth's lawyer, Larry Feldman, accused the pop star of seducing his young client with lavish gifts and attention, then betraying his trust with sexual acts.

"This little boy is going to be vindicated in this court suit," Feldman declared. "That's the reason we brought it, and he deserves it, and I'm going to do everything in my power to make sure that he gets justice whether Michael Jackson likes it or not."

Fields and Pellicano, Jackson's team, noted that the youth was the object of a bitter legal custody battle between his divorced parents. Pellicano said that he had interviewed the boy, who said nothing sexual had transpired between him and Jackson. Pellicano further accused the boy's father of threatening to destroy Jackson's career unless Jackson agreed to buy $20 million worth of screenplays from the boy's father. "The first demands were for money, and the latest demand is for money," Pellicano said dismissively of the civil suit.

Former Jackson household help were already reaping financial rewards from the scandal. Maids, cooks, and bodyguards paraded to the tabloids and for thousands of dollars sold sensational, uncorroborated stories of their former boss's sexual misconduct with children. Pundits criticized the media and police for giving Jackson special treatment. Depending on an analyst's point of view, the "King of Pop" was either being shielded or crucified because of his celebrity.

While the scandal roiled at home, Michael Jackson attempted to maintain his performance schedule abroad. He fell ill and began to miss concert dates. On November 12, he canceled the remainder of his Asian tour and announced that the pressure of the scandal had made him turn to prescription drugs left over from reconstructive surgery, the result of a 1984 accident in which he was severely burned making a Pepsi-Cola commercial. Now addicted to painkillers, Jackson disappeared into an undisclosed clinic for treatment. The media scrambled across Europe looking for him. In California, the alleged victim's attorney demanded that Jackson return to the United States for a deposition.

Jackson's lawyer, Fields, argued that his client should not have to stand trial in the civil suit until the joint criminal investigation by Los Angeles and Santa Barbara District Attorneys offices had run its course. On November 23, however, Jackson was ordered to stand trial in the civil case regardless of the status of the criminal investigation. Jackson's family publicly grumbled that Fields and Pellicano were mishandling the case.

As it was before the scandal, Michael Jackson's real nature remained in the eye of the beholder. Those who suspected him saw a classic psychological profile of a sex offender in his eccentric, reclusive behavior. His defenders cited his philanthropy toward children and saw in his child-like demeanor the perfect target for an extortion attempt. No one ignored the fact that money and Jackson's public image were inextricably linked. Even apart from the sales of his records, videos and concert tickets, profits from product endorsements and film projects involved tens of millions of dollars. Corporations that had profited by Jackson's image now distanced themselves from the besieged star. His record company issued bland statements of support. Pepsi-Cola, sponsor of his canceled concert tour, announced that its long relationship with him was over.

Jackson returned to California in mid-December and was served with a search warrant—for his body. His accuser claimed to be able to identify distinguishing aspects of Jackson's body, including his genitals. These claims would bolster the allegations. Police examined and photographed Jackson's anatomy in great detail.

Jackson described this inspection as "the most humiliating ordeal of my life, one that no person should have to suffer," adding, "if this is what I have to endure to prove my innocence, my complete innocence, so be it."

In an emotional four-minute statement broadcast globally by CNN (Cable News Network) on December 22, 1993, Jackson denied any improper conduct, attributed his postponed return to recovery from his painkiller addiction and accused the mass media of exploiting the "disgusting" charges against him. "I ask all of you to wait and hear the truth before you label or condemn me."

Jackson's defense strategy shifted. Fields and Pellicano resigned from the case. His new lawyers, Howard Weitzman and

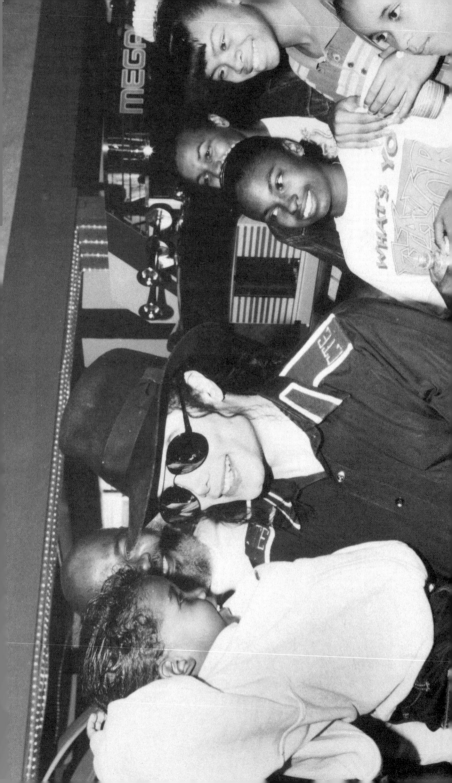

Johnnie Cochran, Jr. (who would later join O.J. Simpson's defense team) began negotiating with the alleged victim's attorney.

In early January 1994, when his accuser's deposition entered the public record, specifics of the complaint against Jackson hit the world press. Jackson's new lawyer, Weitzman downplayed the graphic descriptions of sexual acts, saying, "It's just a plaintiff repeating his allegations, which Mr. Jackson vehemently denies."

Jackson was due to give his own deposition, and the trial was set for March 21. Yet those who wondered if his career and legendary emotional frailty could stand more intrusion never got to hear prosecutors delve into the intimate details of his lifestyle and finances. On January 25, 1994, it was announced that Jackson agreed to settle the civil suit with a reputed payment of over $10 million. Los Angeles District Attorney Gil Garcetti noted that the alleged victim would still be allowed to testify. Since California law does not force victims of sexual misconduct to testify, however, chances of the youth both accepting the large sum and pursuing the complaint seemed unlikely.

"There is no such thing as a classic profile. They made a completely foolish and illogical error," said Dr. Ralph Underwager in an October 1994 interview with *GQ*. The Minneapolis psychiatrist, who has treated pedophiles and victims of incest since 1953, went on to say that he believes Jackson was targeted because of "misconceptions . . . that have been allowed to parade as fact in an era of hysteria."

While onlookers curious about the truth might have felt defeated, attorneys for both sides claimed victory. "The resolution of this case is by no means an admission of guilt by Michael Jackson," his lawyers declared. "He is an innocent man who does not intend to have his career and his life destroyed by rumors and innuendo."

The alleged victim's attorney, Feldman, was equally unyielding. "Nobody has bought anybody's silence," he maintained.

The civil suit was behind him, but prosecutors continued to investigate Jackson for most of the year, interviewing hundreds of witnesses. In September 1994, district attorneys announced that they would not file charges. The unidentified boy who had settled

Rock star Michael Jackson hosts a party for 100 inner-city youths at his ranch in Los Olivos, California, on January 15, 1994.

the civil suit declined to testify. A second possible victim refused to become involved, while a third denied any misconduct by Jackson.

Prosecutors had been willing to proceed with the case until it became clear that the alleged victims were unwilling to participate. The case would remain open, leaving Jackson vulnerable to indictment, if the youth in the initial complaint changed his mind within five years. "We emphasize that our decision is not based on any issue of credibility of the victims," the authorities explained. "Should circumstances change or new evidence develop within the statute of limitations, this decision will be re-evaluated in light of the evidence available at such time."

The prosecutors implied, however, that they assumed the affair to be over. "Michael Jackson is presumed to be innocent as any citizen in this room is if they are not convicted of a crime," Los Angeles District Attorney Garcetti instructed reporters. "We are not charging Michael Jackson with a crime."

Jackson released a brief statement expressing his relief that the investigation was over. He thanked his friends, fans, and family for believing in his innocence. Yet by this time, the scandal and its projected effect on Jackson's career had already been eclipsed by news of his secret marriage to Elvis Presley's daughter, Lisa Marie.

On June 14, 1995, newswoman Diane Sawyer interviewed Michael Jackson and Lisa Marie Presley-Jackson. The much-hyped talk aired on ABC's *PrimeTime Live* opposite the finals in the NBA tournament. More viewers—60 million people—tuned in to see the King of Pop with his bride than to see the Houston Rockets win their second consecutive basketball championship, clearly demonstrating that Jackson's popularity had not suffered from allegations of child abuse. Further, when Jackson released his album *History*, in early July, it went straight to the top of the *Billboard* R&B chart.

—Tom Smith

The tremor felt by tourists at the Statue of Liberty in New York City's harbor on February 26, 1993, was not an earthquake. The shudder reaching across the harbor was the shock of a bomb smashing four underground levels of the World Trade Center, shaking the twin towers of the 110-story complex. Electricity was cut off and elevators stopped, leaving hundreds of office workers and visitors huddling in terror or struggling down dark stairways choked with black smoke.

Six people were killed and more than one thousand were injured by the blast, which resembled terrorist bombings in other parts of the world. The United States had seemed immune from such attacks until this explosion. As a chill of vulnerability touched the nation's cities, investigators crept into the teetering rubble of the center's basement, looking for clues.

Forensic investigators soon determined that the blast was caused by common explosives detonated in a yellow van. They found the charred vehicle's identification number and traced it to a Ryder Rental Company in New Jersey. A few days later, the man who had rented the van told a federal agent posing as a rental clerk that the vehicle had been stolen. When the "clerk" refused to return a $400 deposit, the customer had left in a huff. Federal agents arrested the man at a nearby bus stop and held him without bail.

WANTED BY THE FBI

AIDING & ABETTING; IMPORTATION, MANUFACTURE, DISTRIBUTION AND STORAGE OF EXPLOSIVE MATERIALS

RAMZI AHMED YOUSEF

DESCRIPTION

Date of birth: May 20,1967; Place of birth: Iraq (also claims United Arab Emirates); Height: 6'; Weight: 180 pounds; Build: medium; Hair: brown ; Eyes: brown; Complexion: olive; Sex: male; Race: white; Characteristics: usually clean shaven; Social Security Number Used: 136-94-3472 (invalid SSAN); Aliases: Ramzi Yousef Ahmad, Rasheed Yousef, Ramzi Ahmad Yousef,Kamal Abraham, Muhammud Azan, Ramzi Yousef, Rashid Rashid, Kamal Ibraham, Ramzi Yousef Ahmed, Abraham Kamal, Khurram Khan

CAUTION

YOUSEF ALLEGEDLY PARTICIPATED IN THE TERRORIST BOMBING OF THE WORLD TRADE CENTER, NEW YORK CITY, WHICH RESULTED IN SIX DEATHS, THE WOUNDING OF NUMEROUS INDIVIDUALS, AND THE SIGNIFICANT DESTRUCTION OF PROPERTY AND COMMERCE. YOUSEF SHOULD BE CONSIDERED ARMED AND EXTREMELY DANGEROUS.

April 1993

FBI Wanted Poster April 1993: Ramzi Ahmed Yousef, alleged partaker in the World Trade Center bombing in New York City. Courtesy FBI, Washington, D.C.

The suspect was Mohammed Salameh, a Jordanian living in the United States with an expired tourist visa. Other arrests quickly followed. Nidal Ayyad, a chemical engineer whose business card was discovered in Salameh's pocket, was taken into custody. Bilal Alkaisi, who shared a joint bank account with Salameh and Ayyad, surrendered to the FBI. Alkaisi was charged and later convicted of lying to an immigration officer. A fourth man, Mahmud Abouhalima, was arrested in Cairo and deported to the United States to face indictment. He showed signs of having been tortured by Egyptian police. His American lawyer, William Kunstler, argued unsuccessfully that any admissions by Abouhalima were obtained under duress and should be ruled inadmissible. A fifth suspect, Ibrahim Elgabrowny, was accused of carrying false passports and resisting arrest. He was indicted with Salameh and Ayyad on March 19.

Palestinian Ahmad Ajaj was arrested on May 6, 1993. The previous year, he had been detained at Kennedy International Airport for carrying a tampered passport and military manuals containing bombmaking instructions. After six months of detention, he had been released. When investigators learned that he had traveled to the United States on the same flight as Ramzi Ahmed Yousef, another suspect who had been seen with Salameh in the yellow van, Ajaj was arrested again. Although Yousef's fingerprints were found on the pages of the manuals in Ajaj's luggage, he was nowhere to be found. The FBI placed Yousef on its 10 Most Wanted list, and a $2 million reward was offered for information leading to his arrest.

Ajaj, Ayyad, Salameh, and Abouhalima were charged with a total of 38 crimes, including explosive destruction of property, conspiracy, and interstate transportation of explosives.

SHEIK OMAR ABDEL RAHMAN IS INDICTED

All the suspects except Ajaj were followers of Sheik Omar Abdel Rahman, a blind cleric who preached militant Islam from a Jersey City storefront mosque. Rahman's virulent anti-American sermons attracted a scrutiny by authorities that was lacking before the explosion in New York. He had been acquitted of aiding the 1981 assassination of Egyptian President Anwar Sadat. Fleeing charges of fomenting a riot in his native Egypt, he entered the United States in 1990, despite the fact that his name was on a computer list of suspected terrorists barred from entering the country.

After the World Trade Center bombing, the sheik was constantly surrounded by FBI agents and news hungry reporters. Although it was speculated that he might be arrested for complicity in the bombing, U.S. Attorney General Janet Reno found that too little evidence existed for an immediate indictment.

In late August 1993, however, Rahman and 14 other men were indicted for plotting "a war of urban terrorism against the United States." Under a rarely used seditious conspiracy law, the sheik was charged with guiding the group, whose alleged targets included the United Nations, New York's FBI office, and the Holland and Lincoln Tunnels that connect New York to New Jersey. The defendants were also accused of planning to kill Egyptian President Hosni Mubarak as well as several American politicians sympathetic to Israel. All 15 defendants pleaded not guilty on August 25.

Federal authorities declared that the World Trade Center bombing and other violent acts were part of this wider conspiracy. In a controversial 1991 trial, El Sayyid Nosair had been convicted of gun possession and assault, but acquitted of murdering militant rabbi Meir Kahane in 1990. By claiming that he was involved in the newly uncovered plot, prosecutors were allowed to indict Nosair again for the Kahane murder without breaking the double-jeopardy rule against trying a defendant twice for the same crime. Borrowing a legal tactic used successfully against organized crime figures like John Gotti, the government charged Nosair under the Racketeer

Black Muslim attorneys, (l to r) Clarence Faines, Hassen Ibn Abdellah, and Mohammad Ibn Bashir prepare to enter the Federal Court in Manhattan on September 14, 1993. Together, this defense team represented 33-year-old Egyptian-born Mahmud Abouhalima, one of seven suspects in the World Trade Center bombing. Faye Ellman Photography

Influenced and Corrupt Organizations (RICO) Act, contending that the killing was part of a pattern of criminal activity.

Salameh, Ayyad, Abouhalima, and Ajaj were named as co-conspirators in the World Trade Center bombing case, but no fresh charges were added to those they already faced when their trial began on September 14, 1993, almost seven months after the bombing. Judge Kevin T. Duffy was sufficiently concerned that publicity about the bombing was so pervasive that he ordered an extra five thousand jury duty summonses to be mailed. In fact, a jury was selected in less than a week.

Although none of the accused men had been seen at the sight of the explosion, prosecutors attempted to tie them to the crime by the sheer weight of circumstantial evidence. An entire month crawled by as hundreds of forensic exhibits were introduced in court, ranging from macabre photos of dead victims to dry architectural analyses of the World Trade Center's internal structure.

YELLOW VAN, LETTER TO *THE NEW YORK TIMES,* BOMBMAKING MANUALS

Testimony eventually moved closer to the defendants. Prosecutors produced the frame of a vehicle that experts placed at the very center of the explosion. The serial number on the charred metal matched that of the yellow Ford van rented by Salameh. Bank officers testified that Salameh and Ayyad shared a joint account funded by undetermined overseas sources. A Jersey City, New Jersey, chemical supplier recalled Salameh and the fugitive, Yousef, buying thousands of dollars of raw materials, which experts identified as primary components used in homemade bombs. Other witnesses recalled Ayyad ordering tanks of compressed hydrogen gas, which were delivered to a storage locker rented by Salameh and Yousef. When the storage company personnel asked the renters to remove the tanks, the canisters were picked up by a yellow van.

A gas station attendant recalled two customers filling a yellow van's gas tank on the morning of the blast. When asked to identify the men in court, however, the attendant pointed to two jurors. The witness identified Abouhalima and Salameh when he returned to court the next day. Apart from this wobbly connection, the case against Abouhalima rested almost entirely on sulfuric acid burns on shoes found in his home. Prosecutors noted that the chemical was used in bomb making. Hassen Ibn Abdellah, Abouhalima's attorney, pressed witnesses to admit that the substance could as easily have come from a car battery.

A letter from the Liberation Army Fifth Battalion claiming responsibility for the bomb had been received by *The New York Times* after the blast. DNA testing confirmed a 97 percent probability that Ayyad's saliva had sealed the envelope. No such scientific data was offered in the case against Ajaj. The government contended that Ajaj's possession of military manuals containing bombmaking instructions and Yousef's fingerprints were sufficient proof of his complicity.

Austin Campriello, Ajaj's attorney, argued that the disputed books had helped provoke his client's detention by immigration authorities on September 1, 1992, and could not have been involved in the bombing plot.

"What he slid over," Campriello said, faulting lead Prosecutor J. Gilmore Childers's view of the confiscated manuals, "was that Ahmad's material was taken from him that very day and was in the possession of the U.S. Government until the very day the World Trade Center tragedy occurred."

During four months of testimony from 207 witnesses, defense attorneys (Robert Precht, Atig Ahmed, Hassen Ibn Abdellah, and Austin Campriello) offered no rebuttal witnesses or evidence of their own. None of the defendants testified on his own behalf.

VERDICTS ARE READ

During closing arguments, Salameh's lawyer, Robert Precht, unexpectedly claimed that his client had been manipulated into unwittingly participating in the plot by the fugitive, Yousef. Attorney Precht's gamble did not pay off. After less than a week of deliberation, the defendants were found guilty of all 38 charges.

"Victory to Islam!" Ayyad shouted when the verdict was read.

Timex Keeps on . . . Glowing: Investment adviser Curt Blik used his Timex Ironman Indiglo watch to help find his way though darkness and down 33 flights of stairs after the bombing knocked out power in the World Trade Center.

—*Advertising Age,* March 15, 1993

The defendants dismissed their lawyers while awaiting sentencing. When they returned to court on May 24, 1994, all four were allowed to give statements.

Speaking in Arabic, each defendant protested that the trial was unfair. Salameh, Ayyad, and Abouhalima each gave long, angry political speeches, expressing their distaste for American society and their support for Islamic extremist movements around the globe. Unlike the others, Ajaj called the bombing "a horrible crime." He spoke for over two hours about atrocities committed against the Palestinian people. After witnessing and suffering from such violence, he said, he had no wish to act violently toward anyone.

Judge Duffy eventually cut him off. "All you've done in the past two-and-a-half hours is convince me that anything you say is either a reworking of the truth or an out-and-out lie," Duffy told Ajaj. "You were in this plot up to your ears."

Although all of the crimes tried in the case were serious, none were punishable by life sentences under New York law. When the judge passed sentence, however, it was clear that the convicted men would spend the rest of their lives in prison.

The judge subtracted the ages of each of the six dead victims from an average life expectancy of 60 years. Together, according to this formula, the deceased had been denied a total of 180 years of possible life. To this sum, the judge added mandatory 30-year penalties for each of the two convictions of assault on a federal officer. The defendants were each sentenced to 240 years in prison, with no possibility of parole.

Ajaj planned an appeal with the help of a new court-appointed attorney. A new look was taken at one notebook about explosives, upon which the government had based much of its case. Analysts found that Ajaj's handwriting did not match the incriminating notations in the book.

Ajaj also claimed that he had been planning to mail the other military manuals in his possession to the family of a Jordanian, who had been killed fighting in Afghanistan. He pointed out that the books were only part of a bundle of mail he had agreed to post for other Arabs he met in Pakistan, whose mail links with other countries were not as reliable as those of the U.S. Postal Service. Ajaj admitted that he had met Yousef, but insisted that the fugitive had neither revealed his real name nor spoken of any violent intentions.

THE SECOND TRIAL BEGINS

On January 30, 1995, seven months after the four men convicted of bombing the World Trade Center disappeared into federal prisons, Sheik Abdel Rahman and 10 of his co-defendants went to trial. The prosecution's case was expected to be difficult to prove, for it relied heavily upon the testimony of an Egyptian-born U.S. government informant named Emad Salem, whose credibility and motives were sure to be challenged. As the trial began, however, the defense was shaken by news that Siddig Ibrahim Siddig Ali, the accused mastermind of the plot and Rahman's translator, would plead guilty. Following a plea bargaining agreement, Ali implicated all but one of his co-defendants, including the sheik, whom he accused of approving the bombing targets.

Outraged defense lawyers Lynne Stewart, John Jacobs, Ramsey Clark, and Anthony Ricco protested that Ali's unfolding deal with the government had denied them a chance to attack his credibility in their opening statements. In February, they were demanding a mistrial when even more sensational news broke. On the same day that Ali's plea bargaining was announced, Yousef was arrested in Pakistan. He was being returned to the U.S. to stand trial.

This turn of events presented a new opportunity for the defense lawyers: They could argue that there was only one mastermind behind the bombing and if it was Yousef, then Rahman and his followers could not have done it. The onus was on the Federal prosecutors to prove that there were *two* masterminds, Rahman and Yousef. According to *The New York Times,* this strategy was fine with the lawyers defending Rahman; they reasoned that the more the conspiracy grew around Yousef, the less likely the jury would be to believe that Rahman was guilty of planning the bombing.

Nevertheless, by mid-April U.S. officials had gathered evidence in Denmark that prosecutors believed would link the two men. During a search of the apartments of three of seven Arab men arrested in April 1994 on charges of plotting a bombing of a UN conference in Copenhagen, Danish police discovered bomb manuals, invoices for chemicals, a sketch of terrorist targets in Denmark, videotapes of Abdel Rahman's, and various magazines and pamphlets. The most damning evidence came when it was found that the fingerprints on the manuals and magazines that Ahmad Ajaj (one of the four men convicted in the first trial) was carrying when he entered the United States with Yousef matched those of two of the men arrested in Denmark. Further, prosecutors said that fax and telephone records also suggested that Rahman was communicating with the Danish group before the bombing.

The case, which included 200 witnesses and 100 pieces of evidence, was sent to the jury the third week of September. On Sunday, October 1, the ten defendants were pronounced guilty on 48 of 50 charges. The Sheikh and the nine other militant Muslims on trial were convicted of conspiring to carry out a "war of urban terrorism" intended to force the U.S. to abandon support for Egypt's secular government and for Israel. The jury also convicted El Sayyid Nosair in the 1990 killing of Rabbi Meir Kahane in this second in a trilogy of cases stemming from the World Trade Center bombing.

—Tom Smith

When Lorena Bobbitt picked up a 12-inch fillet knife in her kitchen at 5 A.M. on June 23, 1993, she presumably gave nary a thought to the gift she was about to bestow on the nation's editors and news anchors: The opportunity to put the unmentionable word "penis" in front-page headlines and on network news by the dinner hour. Was it on her mind to focus world attention on the issue of violence against women? Moments later, with one stroke of the knife, she accomplished both results by severing her slumbering husband from his most cherished possession. This act produced two courtroom dramas.

Lorena and John Bobbitt had met, when she was 19 and he was 21, at a club for enlisted men near the Quantico, Virginia, Marine Corps base, where he was a lance corporal. Raised in Venezuela, she was, at the time they met, a manicurist in Manassas, Virginia. She was slender, 5'2", attractive, with long dark brown hair. She held a U.S. immigration visa that was soon to expire.

John was inexperienced with women. Lorena's strict upbringing had included chaperones tagging along on dates, no premarital sex, no tolerance of divorce or abortion. "She was pretty," said John later. "She had a cute accent. We thought we were in love. I didn't want her to leave." They were married on June 18, 1989.

John Wayne Bobbitt poses with Dr. James T. Sehn just three weeks after the urologist successfully performed a nine-hour surgical procedure to reattach Bobbitt's amputated penis. Courtesy James T. Sehn, M.D.

Trouble soon began. John drank. He spent money extravagantly. A month after the wedding, when she criticized his erratic driving, he struck her. When they argued over a television program, he broke off the rooftop antenna, knocked her down with his car, and drove off. In another fight, she locked herself in the bathroom. He unscrewed the doorknob. When she dialed 911, he ripped out the phone. Neighbors noted her recurring bruises. Short of cash, Lorena stole money from her employer and stole dresses from Nordstrom's department store.

Upon completing his Marine enlistment, John began working as a bouncer at a Manassas night club. Over their four-year marriage, interrupted by long separations in 1991 and again in 1992, both Bobbitts called the police to break up their disputes several times. In mid-June 1993, Lorena requested a restraining order against her husband. Two days later, at 3 A.M., he came home drunk.

A house guest, John's buddy Robert Johnston, was asleep in the next room. At about 5 A.M., he felt a kick. He looked up. John Bobbitt, naked, a bloody sheet clutched to his groin, calmly asked Robert to get him to the emergency room. Lorena was not in the house. On the way to the hospital, John said, "They better be able to make me a new penis."

Urologist Dr. James T. Sehn examined Bobbitt, explaining to him that, unless the missing penis was found, he would have to sew the stump closed. With Bobbitt on a gurney ready for surgery, Dr. Sehn pushed him toward the operating room.

At that moment the police arrived at the hospital with the missing organ, packed in ice. They had received a call from Lorena Bobbitt, who told them her husband's penis could be retrieved from a field next to the neighborhood 7-11 convenience store. Dr. Sehn immediately called Dr. David E. Berman, a skilled microsurgeon, and in a nine-hour procedure, they reattached John Bobbitt's penis.

The Life of the Party: In an August 11, 1993, *Wall Street Journal* article, urologist Dr. Sehn admitted that when he would tell strangers about his job, "the conversation would sort of trail off." Not so after he successfully operated on John Wayne Bobbitt. When Sehn arrived at a cocktail party soon after the surgery, he was greeted by spontaneous applause.

LORENA BOBBITT IS CHARGED

Lorena Bobbitt was charged with malicious wounding. Overnight, the amputation, the reattachment, the couple's record of domestic violence, and Lorena's statement, saying she was raped by her drunken husband at 3 A.M., which was the last straw for her, spread like wildfire throughout the world. Late night talk show hosts David Letterman and Jay Leno began quipping Bobbitt jokes night after night.

With Lorena indicted and women's voices rising, Attorney Paul B. Ebert of Prince William County Commonwealth, Virginia, examined Lorena's police statement. Six weeks later, he indicted John Bobbitt on a charge of marital sexual assault.

By this time, the outraged members of the Virginia chapter of the National Organization for Women (NOW) had set up a support hotline. Dr. Sehn's wife was harassed by women who were angry that her husband's surgery had succeeded. "This is a tragedy, not a comedy," said Phyllis D. Barkhurst of the National Coalition Against Domestic Violence. "It is deeply revealing that it has taken the mutilation of a man to attract attention to the abuse of women," said a *New York Times* Op-Ed article.

Both Bobbitts quickly hired agents to handle book and movie offers and public appearances. Almost immediately, Lorena's agents got her on ABC's *20/20*, and in *Vanity Fair* magazine. Both Bobbitts filed for divorce.

JOHN BOBBITT TRIED FOR MALICIOUS ASSAULT

On Monday, November 8, 1993, nine women and three men sat in the jury box in the Prince William County Circuit Court to hear John Wayne Bobbitt tried for malicious assault. Rape was not charged because under Virginia law it applies only to couples living apart or in cases where the victim suffers serious physical injury. Reporters from around the world packed the courtroom. Outside, pushing their way through the hundreds of spectators and reporters who failed to find room inside, hawkers sold nine hundred T-shirts, at $10 each, with the inscription, "Manassas, Va.—A CUT above the rest."

On the witness stand, Lorena Bobbitt tearfully described how her husband had come home drunk, woke her, choked her, and raped her for the second time in two days. "I was crying," she testified. "I said, 'You hurt me again and again and again. How much do I have to put up with?'"

She said Bobbitt then fell asleep. She went to the kitchen to get a drink of water. "The refrigerator door was open," she testified, "and that was the only light. And I turned and saw the knife. I took it. I went to the bedroom. I pulled the sheets off, and I cut him." She said she then ran out, threw the knife into a garbage can, jumped into her car, and drove away. When she realized she still held the penis in her hand, she tossed it into the vacant field next to the convenience store.

Bobbitt took the stand, telling the jury, "I felt a pull, a jerk that hurt real bad and I sprang up—like, silent pain. I grabbed my groin area and held myself." John Bobbitt could not recall whether he had had sex that night. A police detective testified that at the hospital John Bobbitt told him, "if he had sex with his wife, then he may have done it while he was asleep, that he did those things very often."

Stephen Roque, a Prince William County court counselor, told the court that two days before the attack, Lorena Bobbitt had complained of physical and sexual abuse by her husband and had asked about court protection. Told she would have to appear before a judge, she said she would return later in the week.

Called back to the stand, Lorena Bobbitt explained that five days before the attack, her husband had raped her while calling out the names of other women.

In his summation, Prosecutor Ebert said, "You might say these two people deserve each other."

After deliberating for only four hours, the jury found John Bobbitt not guilty. Afterward, a juror said the jury had agreed with John's lawyer, Gregory L. Murphy. The case was too circumstantial, and it could not rely solely on Lorena Bobbitt's word. "If someone had heard her scream," continued the juror, "or if there had been some sort of bruising, that would have made more substantive evidence."

It would be two months before Lorena's trial would begin. Meanwhile, appetites for the sensational were being well fed. Shock jock Howard Stern put John Bobbitt on a New Year's Eve telethon to raise money to defray $250,000 of his legal and medical fees. *People* magazine made the Bobbitts its cover story and devoted five full pages of the same issue to the Bobbitts. Late night talk show hosts Letterman and Leno vied to see who could come up with the most jokes. Feminist author Katie Roiphe wrote in *The New York Times*:

"**If** anything, Lorena could become an anti-role model. With men's reaction so intense, and the media's insistence that she embodies feminism, Lorena could start her very own backlash," columnist and author Cynthia Heimel in *Newsweek*, January 24, 1994.

After Lorena Bobbitt had her husband John Bobbitt arrested for marital sexual assault, she attends his trial at the Prince William County Circuit Court in Manassas, Virginia, on November 8, 1993. *Richmond Times Dispatch*

> Lorena Bobbitt has become a symbol of female rage. . . . With that primal cut, she exposed the raw hostility between the sexes that is usually clothed in everyday social interaction. . . . We need to understand the part of the women's movement that yearns for a Lorena Bobbitt.

LORENA BOBBITT'S TRIAL BEGINS

The trial of Lorena Bobbitt on the felony charge of maliciously wounding her husband opened January 10, 1994. Autographed John Bobbitt T-shirts were selling for $25, all proceeds going to the defense fund. A restaurant offered a Bobbitt Special—a hot dog with French "cut" fries. Downtown Manassas was a mass of eager spectators and throbbing diesels powering satellite trucks.

Seven women and five men occupied the jury box. Prosecutor Ebert's opening statement asserted that, temperamental and demanding, Lorena Bobbitt had acted out of pique.

Defense Attorney Lisa B. Kemler described her client as "a battered woman in the classic sense" who acted in self-defense out of "irresistible impulse," and who was suffering from mental disorders. "What we have," said Kemler, "is Lorena Bobbitt's life juxtaposed against John Wayne Bobbitt's penis. In her mind, it was his penis from which she could not escape. At the end of this case, you will come to one conclusion. And that is that a life is more valuable than a penis."

On the stand, Bobbitt denied he had raped his wife just before the attack. She, he said, had tried to initiate sex when he returned from drinking with a friend, but he was too tired and fell asleep. Then, he testified, "I was bleeding. I hurt real bad. I thought she just, you know, grabbed me, just pulled it out of my body."

Defense witnesses testified to John's boasting that he enjoyed brutal sex with women, repeatedly hit his wife, pulled her hair, and threw her against the wall.

Lorena's defense traced the disintegration of the Bobbitts's marriage, the increasing violence, and John Bobbitt's use of what she called "Marine Corps torture techniques," which included twisting her leg so severely that she was hospitalized. She finally acted, said James Lose, one of her defense lawyers, on "irresistible impulse," a form of temporary insanity.

In cross-examination, Lorena testified that she did not remember severing John's penis. Only when she found it in her hand while driving away, she said, did she realize what she had done. But Assistant Commonwealth Attorney Mary Grace O'Brien retorted by quoting Lorena's police statement. "He always have orgasm and he doesn't wait for me to have orgasm," it said. "He's selfish. I don't think it's fair, so I pulled back the sheets then and I did it."

Attorney O'Brien then asked Lorena, "You're saying under oath that you don't remember cutting him?"

"No," said Lorena. "That's what I assumed happened."

A defense psychiatrist testified that Lorena suffered a "brief reactive psychosis" under which she attacked "the instrument that was the weapon of her torture." A prosecution psychiatrist rebutted by declaring, "she had a choice to make. She chose to amputate that penis, and as such we do not have an irresistible impulse but an impulse she did not resist."

After six hours of deliberation, the jury concluded that Lorena Bobbitt was temporarily insane when she cut off her husband's penis. It found her not guilty on all criminal charges. Said a male member of the jury, "We didn't believe John Bobbitt."

Under state law, Lorena underwent five weeks of psychiatric examination in a mental hospital and was released.

JOHN BOBBITT'S TROUBLES CONTINUE

The press announced that John Bobbitt was booked on a worldwide media tour billed as "Love Hurts." Within months, he was engaged to marry a former topless dancer, Kristina Elliott. But on May 6, 1994, in Las Vegas, Elliott had Bobbitt arrested for assault, asserting that he had thrown her against a wall. He pleaded not guilty. Out on bail and awaiting trial, he announced complete recovery from his celebrated surgery. "It's like it was before," he said. "There's no problem."

June found Bobbitt in court again in a paternity suit. He pleaded guilty and arranged a settlement with Beatrice L. Williams of Niagara Falls, New York. He said he was "thrilled, excited and blessed" to be the father of a 17-month-old son. Two months later, he was convicted of a misdemeanor against Kristina Elliott, his former fiancee. Observing that Bobbitt had "an attitude problem," Las Vegas Justice of the Peace William Jansen sentenced him to 60 days in jail, then suspended 45 of the days. "Your attitude problem is caused by your drinking," said the judge. He ordered therapy and membership in Alcoholics Anonymous, as John Wayne Bobbitt was led from the courtroom to jail.

In 1994 John Bobbitt starred in an X-rated movie with an all-too predictable title: "John Wayne Bobbitt Uncut."

Releasing Lorena Bobbitt after psychiatric evaluation in a mental health facility, Prince William County Circuit Court Judge Herman A. Whisenant, Jr., ordered her to undergo outpatient treatment weekly and not to leave Virginia without permission. She resumed her career as a manicurist.

—Bernard Ryan, Jr.

As the 1994 Winter Olympics drew near, Nancy Kerrigan and Tonya Harding were likely contenders in the women's figure skating contest. Strong rivals, they both expected to be named to the U.S. team and to reach the finals in the competition for gold, silver, and bronze medals.

Although Kerrigan had won the bronze in the 1992 Olympics, she performed poorly during most of 1993. Toward the end of 1993, she made a strong comeback by finishing first in the U.S. Championships and fifth in the World Championships.

On January 6, 1994, Kerrigan finished a strenuous practice session for the 1994 U.S. Figure Skating Championships that would be opening the next day in Cobo Hall, Detroit. She stepped through the gate, off the ice, and, still wearing her skates, walked through the crowd of onlookers toward the locker room. Suddenly she felt a violent blow to her right knee. Falling backward, she screamed, "Why me?" A couple of witnesses caught only a glimpse of her assailant before he disappeared. Almost immediately Detroit police and the FBI began investigating.

Kerrigan was taken to the hospital, where X-rays revealed no broken bones, but her right leg—the one on which she landed in her jumps—was severely bruised. She couldn't skate. Saying she was "upset and angry," she withdrew from the U.S. competition, even

Tonya Harding skates at the 1994 U.S. Figure Skating Championship on January 7, 1994, at Cobo Hall in Detroit, Michigan, where rival Nancy Kerrigan was wounded off the ice by an assailant. Harding went on to win the title for the U.S. women's figure skating event.

Alan Lessig/*Detroit News*

though a top showing was a prerequisite for a position on the U.S. Olympic team. She hoped the Olympic Committee would grant her a waiver. As potential teammates said they would accept such a waiver, Tonya Harding won the U.S. women's figure skating championship, securing a place on the Olympic team. Kerrigan got her wish and was also named to the team.

On January 13, 1994, in Tonya Harding's home town of Portland, Oregon, police arrested her bodyguard, Shawn Eric Eckardt, and Derrick B. Smith, a resident of Phoenix, Arizona, who was then unemployed, on charges of conspiracy in the attack on Kerrigan. Jeff Gillooly, Harding's former husband (with whom she had recently resumed living), admitted to an Oregon newspaper reporter that he was under police investigation, but he denied any involvement. Since the authorities said they had no plans to charge Tonya Harding, the U.S. Olympic Committee said it would keep her on the team.

Why did the authorities suspect a conspiracy that involved Harding? The winner of the Olympic gold medal in figure skating could expect to earn $10 to $15 million by making appearances and endorsing commercial products. Additionally, Harding was known to be tough, aggressive, and desperate for money: She had fought with a husband who abused her; she had hired a bodyguard with a criminal record; and she had recently fired her manager despite his ability to bring in profitable endorsement contracts. Other skaters considered her pushy and she was noted for a violent temper and an absolute determination to win the Olympic gold. She alone among American skaters had landed a triple-Axel spin in competition. According to police, Harding had displayed her temper by taking a baseball bat from her pickup truck to confront a woman in a traffic dispute. Throughout her on-again, off-again relationship with Jeff Gillooly, she had had money problems. Four months earlier, they had been evicted from their apartment by court order for not paying the rent. When reporters asked what she thought about the Olympics, Harding said, "To be perfectly honest, what I'm thinking about are dollar signs."

Sports columnists mused. Talk shows buzzed. The U.S. Olympic Committee met in special session in Durham, North Carolina, to consider removing Harding from the squad bound for Lillehammer, Norway, in February 1994. It decided that, since she had not been implicated in the bashing of Kerrigan's knee, it had no legal grounds for removing her. Meanwhile, as Michigan and Oregon prosecutors continued investigating how and why Nancy Kerrigan had fallen, her bruised knee was mending and she resumed practice sessions on the ice.

POLICE INTERROGATE HARDING

On January 18, twelve days after Kerrigan's injury, investigators in Portland interrogated Harding for nine hours during which she steadfastly denied any part in the assault on her rival skater. The next day, federal authorities arrested ex-husband Gillooly because bodyguard Eckardt had revealed that Gillooly told them Harding knew in advance about the conspiracy to assault Kerrigan. Harding immediately denied any involvement and again split with Gillooly. Around the country, sports columnists urged the Olympic Committee to remove Harding from the team. The U.S. Figure Skating Association began to consider disciplinary action against her. Rumors flew that Gillooly was meeting with state and federal authorities to plea bargain.

Tonya Harding called a news conference on January 27 to read a statement admitting that she had found out a few days after the assault that "persons that were close to me" were involved. Criticizing herself for the delay in telling the authorities, she said, "I am embarrassed and ashamed to think that anyone close to me could be involved," and she apologized to Kerrigan. Her statement concluded:

Nancy Kerrigan and I can show the world two different types of figure skating. . . . I look forward to being on the team with her. I have devoted my entire life to one objective: winning an Olympic gold medal for my country. This is my last chance. I ask only for your understanding and the opportunity to represent my country with the best figure skating performance of my life.

More Fodder for Dave: In February 1994 alone, the name Gillooly had appeared in no fewer than 10 Top Ten Lists on *Late Night with David Letterman.*

The U.S. Olympic Committee named a special five-member panel to investigate Harding's involvement in the assault and to consider disciplinary action. Spectators gathered four-deep around the rink where Harding practiced daily. Meanwhile, Gillooly's lawyer, Ronald H. Hoevet, revealed that Harding had helped plan the attack and given final approval before it occurred. Telephone logs and bank records, said Hoevet, would corroborate his charges.

GILLOOLY PLEADS GUILTY, IMPLICATES HARDING

On February 1, Gillooly pleaded guilty to the assault charge and testified that Harding, his ex-wife, helped plan the attack on Kerrigan. Under the terms of the plea bargain, Gillooly received a two-year jail sentence and was fined $100,000 on a single count of racketeering, but he also received a guarantee that he would not be prosecuted on any other state or federal charges.

On the same day, the special five-member panel met in Colorado Springs but did not come to a decision. For the next week and a half, until the Winter Games opened on February 12, hearsay and circumstantial evidence swirled before columnists, commentators, and the public.

On February 5, the special five-member panel recommended that Tonya Harding be called to a disciplinary hearing by the U.S. Olympic Committee (USOC). Before setting a date, the committee warned her that she might be called before the administrative board of the games in Norway. The International Olympic Committee then announced that it would support whatever the USOC decided. The USOC scheduled a hearing for February 15, which would be four days into the games. On February 9, Harding's lawyer, Robert C. Weaver, Jr., appeared in the Clackamas County Circuit Court, Oregon, to request a temporary restraining order to delay the committee's hearing. At the same time, he filed a lawsuit against the committee. The suit sought $20 million in punitive damages and $5 million in compensatory damages for the committee's "maliciously" interfering with Harding's training and damaging her reputation and earning power. It also asked for a permanent injunction to prevent the committee from interfering in her participation in the Olympics. Gillooly, meanwhile, tried to get permission to attend the hearing so he could testify against his ex-wife.

THE OLYMPICS

The dust seemed to settle on February 12, opening day of the Olympics in Lillehammer, Norway. In an out-of-court agreement, the USOC canceled its hearing and Harding dropped her suit. Harding was now cleared to skate and Olympic officials were relieved. The news media and TV broadcasters predicted top ratings for the women's figure-skating events. On February 12, Harding, climbing into her truck outside her Portland apartment, told reporters, "I finally get to prove to the world I can win a gold medal."

In Norway, Nancy Kerrigan took first place in the semifinals while Tonya Harding, stumbling out of her triple lutz and failing to complete two of eight required elements, dropped to tenth. The next day in the finals, she interrupted her performance to swing one leg up onto the rink wall to show the judges there was a defective lace in one skate. They rescheduled her to skate last. When the program ended, Harding was in eighth place and Kerrigan had won the silver medal, having been edged out by gold medalist Oksana Baiul of Ukraine.

With the world figure skating championships in Japan scheduled for March, Tonya Harding obtained a temporary restraining order on March 9. U.S. District Judge Owen Panner barred the U.S. Figure Skating Association from holding its disciplinary hearing, thus freeing

> "**I** was looking at [prison] as a vacation from all the hassles"
>
> —imprisoned bodyguard Shawn Eckardt on why he didn't want to join Jeff Gillooly in a prison boot camp, quoted in *Sports Illustrated,* September 26, 1994.

Harding to compete in the world championships. The association decided not to appeal. The judge set June 27 for the hearing.

HARDING ADMITS GUILT

Everything changed on March 16, 1994, when Judge Donald H. Londer of the Multnomah County District Court in Portland, Oregon, accepted a plea bargain from Tonya Harding, who pleaded guilty to conspiring to hinder the prosecution for Kerrigan—a felony offense. "Her indictment," said Deputy District Attorney Norman W. Frink, "would have led to a prolonged disrupted media frenzy that would have tied up the court and this office for a year." While she might have been convicted on more serious charges, Frink added, her guilty plea on this single count would insure that justice was served. She would serve no prison time, but would have to put in five hundred hours of community service, spend three years on probation, undergo a psychiatric examination, and resign from the U.S. Figure Skating Association, thus losing her eligibility for the world championships in Japan the following week. She would also have to pay a $100,000 fine, contribute $50,000 to establish a fund for Special Olympics in Oregon, and reimburse the county $50,000 for legal expenses. Meanwhile, the skater continued to hold to her position that she found out about the assault only after it happened and just did not tell the authorities what she knew.

The next day, despite the fact that Harding's plea bargain had included her resignation from the U.S. Figure Skating Association, the association decided "tentatively" that it would hold a disciplinary hearing against her in late June. A week later, when her bodyguard and his accomplices were indicted on charges of racketeering, conspiracy to commit assault, and second-degree assault, Harding was identified as an "unindicted co-conspirator."

In May, after they each pleaded guilty to the lesser charge of conspiracy to commit assault, the men were sentenced to 18 months in prison. As agreed in his plea bargain, Harding's ex-husband served two years.

U.S. FIGURE SKATING ASSOCIATION BANS HARDING

On the last day of June 1994, the U.S. Figure Skating Association's five-member disciplinary panel banned Tonya Harding from the association for life and took away the national championship she had won in Detroit six months earlier.

Under her three-year probation, Harding went to work mowing lawns and planting shrubs for a landscaping company in Portland. To help pay her legal bills, she made an appearance at a professional wrestling match (for an undisclosed sum, and without wrestling), sold TV rights to her life story for $50,000, and made her acting debut in the low-budget Hollywood feature film, *Breakaway.*

—Bernard Ryan, Jr.

TONYA HARDING

KENNETH LEE PEACOCK CASE

arried life did not go smoothly for Kenneth and Sandra Peacock. After seven years of marriage, they moved from east Texas to Parkton, Maryland, just north of the Gunpowder River. That was the spring of 1993. The trouble between them ended on February 9, 1994.

Truck driver Kenneth Lee Peacock started a long-distance haul to Florida that day, but a winter storm covered the interstate highways with ice. He tried to call his wife Sandy because he wanted to tell her that he was not making the run south. No one picked up the receiver. A few hours later, the roads were still icy but navigable enough for Ken to drive home. He tried to call a second time to tell Sandy he was coming home, but there was no answer. When he returned to the darkened house around midnight, he found his wife in bed with another man, drunk, naked, and asleep.

Peacock smacked the stranger awake with the barrel of his deer rifle. After the stranger stumbled out of the house, the Peacocks quarreled into the night. Sandy called her mother in Texas and said she would be coming home. Ken took the phone. "She's lucky I'm letting her live to leave," he said.

Shortly after 4 A.M., after hours of heavy drinking and bitter arguments, Peacock pulled the trigger on his rifle and fired a single shot at Sandy's head, killing her.

Every year about 1,500 women are killed by a male partner or spouse. Sandra Peacock might well have become a forgotten statistic in this bloody toll. As it turned out, a furor over the penalty her husband would pay for taking her life grew far louder than any shock felt over the killing itself.

Peacock called 911 to report that he had shot his wife because she was "sleeping around." When police and paramedics arrived, they found her dead on the sofa. Peacock said to police that he had been trying to scare her with the rifle, but he claimed it had discharged accidentally. He said that he had drunk a gallon of wine and several beers in the hours before the shooting. He was charged with second-degree murder.

At first, there was very little about the Peacock case to differentiate it from other fatal cases of domestic violence, particularly those involving alcohol. Both Peacocks had drinking problems. After Ken was released on bail, Sandy's mother visited him. He told her that the killing was an accident. She forgave him.

LEGALLY ADEQUATE PROVOCATION?

In an effort to reduce the charge against his client, Peacock's attorney, David B. Irwin, attempted plea bargaining. Given the circumstances in which Peacock had discovered his spouse, Irwin argued that his client's actions met Maryland's standard of "legally adequate provocation" and so Peacock was eligible for the reduced charge of voluntary manslaughter instead of premeditated murder.

After weighing the evidence, taking into account Peacock's alcoholism, and consulting with Sandy's parents, state prosecutors agreed to drop the second-degree murder charge if Peacock would plead guilty to first-degree voluntary manslaughter. In effect, he would be accepting punishment for causing his wife's death in return for the state's agreement not to prosecute him on the more serious charge of intentionally murdering her. He agreed. All that seemed to remain was for a sentence to be imposed in open court.

On October 17, 1994, Peacock pleaded guilty to first-degree voluntary manslaughter before Baltimore County Circuit Judge Robert E. Cahill, Sr. Defense Attorney Irwin told the court that his client was a hard worker with no previous criminal record, who had acted in the heat of passion. He pointed out that Sandra Peacock's drinking, gambling, and past marital infidelities had cost her the

Circuit Court Judge Robert Cahill presents his point of view to Judge J. Norris Byrnes during a round table discussion prior to Cahill's bid for reelection in 1992. As the presiding judge in the Ken Peacock trial, Cahill sentenced Peacock, who pleaded guilty to a reduced charge of voluntary manslaughter in the shooting of his wife Sandra, to a minimum 3-year sentence, then suspended half of that. Cahill's lenient sentence was highly criticized, especially by women's groups. David Hobby, *Towson Times*

custody of her children from previous marriages. Irwin added that Kenneth Peacock's family—including two veteran Baltimore County police officers—were sitting in the courtroom as a gesture of support.

PEACOCK GETS LIGHT SENTENCE

Sandra Peacock's family had not come from Texas to witness the trial. Once prosecutors had the family's assurance that a plea bargain was acceptable, the case was pursued as a domestic abuse killing. While the penalty would ultimately be decided under the judge's discretion, Assistant State Attorney Michael G. DeHaven asked for the customary three-to-eight-year term set forth in Maryland's state sentencing guidelines.

"Three-to-eight-years for a first offender is a heavy sentence," replied Judge Cahill after the lawyers had completed their statements. The judge recalled cases in which he had sentenced drunk drivers whose guilt was compounded by the fact that their negligence had killed their own friends or family members. In this case, Cahill reflected that he had the minor comfort of making a decision without the victim's family watching.

"The courtroom contains visitors on only one side, so I get the benefit of sentencing in anonymity," Cahill said. "There is a good chance that this case will not even be written up."

As Cahill spoke, it became increasingly evident that Peacock would have walked free from court that day if it were up to the 62-year-old jurist. "I seriously wonder how many men married five, four years would have the strength to walk away without inflicting some corporal punishment," Judge Cahill said, speaking of Mrs. Peacock's infidelity. "I shudder to think what I would do," Judge Cahill reflected, placing himself in the cuckolded defendant's shoes. "I'm not known for having the quietest disposition."

"I'm forced to impose a sentence," added the judge, "only because I think I must do it to make the system honest."

Cahill sentenced Peacock to three years, to be suspended after 18 months. However, Peacock would spend no time in prison. Under a work release program, he would be able to continue working while spending his non-labor hours in the Baltimore County Detention Center, a local facility. He was ordered to undergo counseling for his alcoholism. He was not required to undergo any domestic violence counseling, but was ordered to perform 50 hours of unspecified community service for a local domestic violence program.

TEMPEST RAGES OVER JUDGE CAHILL'S SENTENCING

An uproar began as word spread that the judge had sentenced a man to only a year-and-a-half for killing his wife, and that the judge had virtually apologized for sentencing the man to any time at all. Everything about the case—from Judge Cahill's competence to the concept of equal justice under the law—suddenly fell under severe public scrutiny. Critics of the Peacock sentence were especially stung when, only one day after the Peacock decision, another Baltimore judge sent a Maryland woman to prison for killing a husband who had beaten her for years.

Stunned critics questioned why state prosecutors had agreed to plea bargaining based on the premise that Peacock had acted "in the heat of passion," when four hours had elapsed between Peacock's discovery of his wife's unfaithfulness and the fatal shot. Others felt that the judge's remarks reflected the insensitivity of Maryland's judicial system itself, whose ranks were disproportionately dominated by older white males. Women's advocacy groups across the country were outraged and demanded Judge Cahill's removal from the bench. With no binding commission to discipline its own members, Maryland's judiciary could offer no redress for the judge's insensitive words.

Complaints came from unexpected quarters. A felon serving a 20-year sentence for attempted murder complained publicly that his jail time was arbitrarily long compared to the Peacock sentence, especially since the woman he had shot had survived.

"**Judge Robert E. Cahill has probably been added to the 'They Just Don't Get It' hall of fame,"** Mercy for a Cuckolded Killer, *Washington Post*, October 19, 1994.

Publicity about the case reached far beyond Maryland, contrary to Judge Cahill's offhanded assumption that the fatal incident would "not even be written up." *The New York Times* called the judge's sentencing remarks "loony." Describing the judge's words as "truly stupid," columnist Anna Quindlen pondered the implications of maligning the victims of domestic murders, rather than those who commit them.

"This week," Quindlen wrote, "the equation was two fold: female infidelity [sic] twice as bad as male abuse, the life of a woman [sic] half as valuable as that of a man. The killing of the woman taken in adultery has a long history and survives today in many cultures. One of those cultures is our own."

Death threats dogged Judge Cahill, who refused to talk to the press and traveled only with the protection of armed guards. Angry protesters and television crews trailed him for weeks, but he remained ensconced on a Baltimore County circuit court bench.

While the moral tempest provoked by the Peacock case raged, those who had been closest to the victim, Sandra Peacock, said their piece but then quickly faded from view. Her parents were unhappy with Ken Peacock's light sentence. They had expected a longer prison term, but also seemed inclined to forgive their son-in-law. Mary Lemon, the victim's mother, blamed alcohol for destroying both Sandy's and Ken's lives.

Less than two weeks after the controversial sentence was imposed upon Ken Peacock, he was hauling freight again, alone with his memories in the cab of a truck.

Judge Cahill is still on the bench.

—Tom Smith

In December 1992, a Pandora's box was opened when a burglar pocketed the jewelry of Elizabeth Adams, a.k.a. Madame Alex, a retired procuress who had been arrested numerous times for pimping to Hollywood's rich and famous. Reading about the ongoing investigation in the *Los Angeles Times,* Los Angeles vice police became riled when they noticed a quote from a young woman declaring herself to be Madam Alex's protégé and successor in the business of providing expensive Hollywood call girls to businessmen. "What it took her years to build, I built in one," bragged the anonymous woman.

By the spring of 1993, undercover Police Detective Sammy Lee was chummily negotiating with the boastful madam, 27-year-old Heidi Fleiss, who promised that she could easily arrange "entertainment" for visiting Japanese businessmen. Hidden police video and audio tapes rolled in a Beverly Hilton Hotel suite as Fleiss boasted of the high quality of her call girls and efficiently laid out the prix fixe of $1,500 she charged each customer.

"In the history of this business, no one has ever been able to do what I do," Fleiss told Lee, who asked if Fleiss could provide cocaine along with sex partners. She told him that would be no problem.

When four women showed up at a hotel suite and disrobed for the arranged "party" on the night of June 8, 1993, they were arrested by undercover detectives. Soon thereafter, police arrived at Fleiss's home and arrested her for felony pimping, pandering, and possession of 13 grams of cocaine. Police also confiscated address books, allegedly full of the names of Fleiss's clients and details of their transactions. Reporters, who swarmed around the stylishly dressed "Hollywood Madam" at her August 9, 1993, arraignment, spoke of the six seized address books as one apocryphal "little black book" capable of incinerating scores of Hollywood reputations.

For a successful person in a role that customarily thrives on discretion, Fleiss was amazingly talkative after she was released on $100,000 bail. She spoke freely to the press of her business strategies. Dropping a few prominent names, she promised to have plenty to say about her customers, who allegedly included international businessmen, rock stars, and famous actors. The select few she named denied any involvement with her. One male Columbia Pictures vice president issued a public statement denying doing any business with Fleiss. Oddly enough, no one had accused him of having done so. Rock star Billy Idol issued a more bemused denial. "I have never used her professional services, and God knows I don't need to," the singer responded. "Fortunately, I've never had to pay for sex."

Far more serious than titillating speculation about the identity of Fleiss's clients, however, was a rumor that major Hollywood film studios had used her services when they needed an enticement to close business deals. If it could be proven or even convincingly alleged that film development money had been diverted from studio budgets to buy prostitutes and drugs, powerful heads might roll. In a more Machiavellian cast, if such rumors gathered enough credence, they might also be effectively used as blackmail or as a public relations wrecking ball to ruin the personal lives and professional reputations of competing executives or even whole studios.

The juicy rumors became so animated that national tabloids portrayed Hollywood's rich and powerful male executives holding their breath to see if anyone would talk. Would Heidi tell all? Would the Los Angeles Police Department disclose the names in her "black book"?

Fleiss exploited her new celebrity status like a pro. She launched a line of designer sleepwear and undergarments bearing her own name and opened a store in Pasadena, California. She seldom stopped talking; yet, when it became clear that the police were not going to release the contents of her ledgers, most of the world stopped listening.

As Fleiss faded from the front page, her problems increased. On July 28, 1994, she and her prosperous pediatrician father Dr. Paul Fleiss were indicted on 14 counts of conspiracy, tax fraud, and money laundering. The Internal Revenue Service wondered how "personnel consultant" Heidi Fleiss was managing to live in a $1.6 million mansion while reporting less than $50,000 in annual income. The Fleisses, who pleaded not guilty on August 1, were charged with funneling Heidi's prostitution profits into a bank account registered in her sister Shana's name. Shana Fleiss was reportedly unaware of the scheme and was not charged. Heidi tested positive for drug use and was ordered to undergo treatment for violating the terms of her bail agreement on September 19.

Once an entrepreneur, always an entrepreneur: In September 1993, in an appearance on the Joan Rivers' show, Fleiss announced that she was beginning a mail-order business for a line of sleepwear she designed, appropriately branded HeidiWear. In July 1994 she opened a boutique in Pasadena, California, to sell the expanded collection. —*People,* August 8, 1994

Meanwhile, Fleiss's arrest and the police decision not to expose the vaguely-worded contents of the "black book" continued to fuel debate. Was the case a grudge match between the police and a self-promoting pimp? Civil libertarians, arguing that prostitution is a victimless crime, squared off against vice detectives and prosecutors, who deplored a manipulative traffic in human lives. Taxpayers in a metropolis wracked with gang warfare wondered why the police were wasting time and money chasing high-priced hookers.

The Fleiss trial, which began on November 14, was not the spectacle some expected. No reputations were ruined nor did Hollywood studios crumble. Instead, the trial reflected a more familiar moral debate over whether prostitutes and pimps should be prosecuted if their customers are allowed to go free.

Fleiss's attorney, Anthony Brooklier argued that she had been entrapped by detectives. He maintained the trial was dominated by an unfair double standard. If the customers in Fleiss's ledgers were not going to be indicted, Brooklier saw no reason his client should be threatened with conviction. "This," said Brooklier, "is hypocrisy at its best."

Los Angeles County Superior Court Justice Judith Champagne, however, ruled that the names in the "black book" and the police decision not to charge Fleiss's customers were irrelevant to the case. After the judge's decision, the trial became an unstoppable parade of prosecution evidence.

Samantha Burdette, one of Fleiss's "girls," explained the percentage she would pay Fleiss for arranging work as a prostitute. Burdette described handing Detective Lee the cocaine he had requested as part of the sexual package deal, shortly before 20 police officers burst into the hotel suite to bust the "party." The arrest was captured on videotape and shown to the jury. Video and audio tapes of Fleiss's meetings and telephone conversations with Lee devastated the defense.

"This is not a complicated case," said Deputy District Attorney Alan Carter in the prosecution's final argument.

When the jurors returned on December 2, after four days of deliberating, they acquitted Fleiss on the drug possession charge and declared that they were deadlocked on two counts of pandering. On the remaining three pandering counts, however, Fleiss was found guilty. Under California law, she faced a mandatory three-year sentence for the convictions.

Fleiss looked stunned. Her hand went to her heart. A moment later, she wilted over the defense table in shock. She was not the only one dismayed by the verdict. Members of the jury began to speak openly of their fractious, noisy deliberations. The verdicts had been reached only after angry disputes over the suitability of the charges. With the trial behind them, the forewoman and several other jurors were openly critical of the police investigation and declared the verdict should be overturned. Two of the jurors told the press they never would have voted to convict Fleiss if they had known of the mandatory three-year prison term accompanying the pandering convictions. Furthermore, the Fleiss jurors admitted that some of their haggling had involved trading votes. To reach a verdict, several jurors had only agreed to vote for convictions on pandering counts in exchange for one juror's acquittal vote on the cocaine possession charge.

In California, possible penalties for criminal acts are not supposed to be discussed during deliberations over guilt or innocence. Fleiss's attorney wasted no time filing an appeal. Brooklier accused the jury of "horse-trading" and challenged the verdict on grounds of juror misconduct.

Fleiss was due to be sentenced on January 20, 1995. Before sentences could be passed, however, Brooklier's co-counsel Donald Marks asked that five of the jurors be granted immunity from prosecution. The immunity freed the jurors to testify that they had discussed Fleiss's possible penalties while arguing over the verdict.

"If they didn't consider penalties, it would have been a hung jury," concluded Marks. "She wouldn't have been convicted."

After an investigation of the jury's behavior, however, Fleiss lost her bid for a new trial on March 24. In denying Attorney Marks's motion for retrial, Judge Champagne agreed that the jurors had engaged in misconduct. Nevertheless, the judge found that the jury's misbehavior was insufficient to prejudice the decision against the defendant.

"The jury system is fundamentally human," Judge Champagne said. "It is an impossible standard to require the jury to be a laboratory."

On May 24, Fleiss was sentenced to the minimum statutory term of three years in prison and was fined $1,500. She immediately filed an appeal. On August 10, the Hollywood madam was also convicted of hiding hundreds of thousands of dollars in earnings from her call-girl ring. A federal jury found Fleiss guilty of conspiracy, tax evasion, and money laundering. Sentencing was set for November 13. Fleiss faces a maximum of five years in prison (in addition to the three years she was sentenced to by the state court). She may also be required to forfeit cash and property.

Fleiss's case was an unusual reversal of a common 1990s scenario in which trials for serious crimes frequently degenerate into media circuses. In her case, the spectacle came first and later faded into legal arguments.

—Tom Smith

Hollywood's Heidi Fleiss smiles for the cameras as she faces pandering and drug distribution charges at the Los Angeles Courthouse on August 9, 1993. Fleiss pleaded not guilty on all counts.

TUPAC SHAKUR CASE

Gangsta rap, as its practitioners and aficionados call it, is a rhythmic, chantlike musical genre with lyrics that often glorify guns, drugs, and violence. The degradation of women has been a recurrent rap theme, particularly in the songs of Tupac Shakur, known to his fans as the king of "gangsta rap."

Critics of Shakur's music claim that his lyrics encourage violence, citing a case in which a young man gunned down a Texas state trooper and later told authorities that Shakur's music had inspired his action. Running for re-election in 1992, Vice President Dan Quayle urged record store chains to stop selling Shakur's album *2Pacalypse Now* on the grounds that its lyrics condoned violence against the police. Although a number of stores agreed, the rapper's music remained as popular as ever; and so much so that he began a film career, co-starring with Janet Jackson in *Poetic Justice* and starring in *Above the Rim*.

Whether out of personal inclination or a shrewd publicity sense, Shakur reveled in his badboy reputation, once describing himself as the "hardest prick out there" and having the words "thug life" tattooed across his chest. Dismissing his critics, Shakur and his defenders argued that his music was merely a reflection of the cruel reality of the mean streets in America's inner cities.

In Shakur's case whether art imitates life or life imitates art has been an open question since 1992 when he had the first of several highly publicized and increasingly serious run-ins with the law. He was cleared of charges arising out of a 1993 gunfight with two off-duty police officers on the streets of Atlanta, Georgia, but in 1994 he was convicted of attacking a man with a baseball bat at a 1993 concert in East Lansing, Michigan.

In November 1994 Shakur was arrested after a 19-year-old fan reported to police that she was with the performer in a New York hotel room when several of his friends came in and, led by Shakur, forced her to perform oral sex on them. Shakur and his road manager, Charles Fuller, were charged with three counts of first degree sexual abuse, sodomy, and illegal possession of a firearm after police found two guns in the rapper's hotel room. (One of the other two men involved was not apprehended and the fourth faced a separate trial.)

From the beginning of Shakur's trial, which began in New York City almost one year after the incident had happened, everyone involved seemed to expect a sleazy and dramatic courtroom battle. First, two jurors had to be removed by Justice Daniel P. Fitzgerald because they had been overheard voicing their disgust with the defendant and his music. Replacing two jurors was a minor procedural hurdle for the court, but it was an omen of things to come.

SHAKUR'S ACCUSER TAKES THE STAND

Assistant District Attorney Francine James began the state's case against Shakur and his three co-defendants by calling his accuser to the stand. (As is often the case in rape or sexual assault cases, the media did not report the victim's name in an effort to protect her privacy.) She told the jury that she had met Shakur at a Manhattan nightclub several days before the alleged attack. During this first encounter, she acknowledged performing oral sex on Shakur, just half an hour after meeting the rap star. Later, the two returned to Shakur's hotel suite for the night. She testified that she called the rapper's voice mail the next day to compliment him on his sexual prowess from the night before.

Four days after this first encounter, she returned to the rapper's hotel suite to retrieve something she had left there. She testified that she and Shakur had been in his room kissing when three of

Rap star Tupac Shakur prepares to enter the Manhattan Supreme Court in New York City on December 1, 1994, after he was shot during an alleged robbery the previous night. He was anticipating a verdict from the jury, which was still deliberating his case. AP/Wide World Photos

his friends burst in and attacked her. Shakur grabbed her by the hair and began tearing her clothes off, while the other three fondled her, she told the jury. Earlier, in a statement given to prosecutors, she had quoted Shakur as telling her that she was "a reward for his friends" and that "millions of other women would be happy to be in her situation." During cross-examination the defense attacked the victim's story.

The defense called only one witness, Shakur's publicist, Talibah Mbonisi. She testified that on the night in question, she had returned to the hotel suite and was told that Shakur was with a woman; she heard no noises coming from the adjoining room. Some time later, according to her testimony, Shakur entered the adjoining room and was talking to Mbonisi when the victim burst in and demanded to know who he was with and why had he just had sex with her if he had someone else waiting for him.

Shakur later told reporters that his accuser was out to get him because she had seen him with another woman. Defense Attorney Michael Warren used the same theory in his argument to the jury, contending that the second sexual encounter with the rap star was as consensual as the first and that the allegations were made to punish the rap star for spurning her.

The judge charged the jury, defining the elements necessary for each offense, the definition of beyond a reasonable doubt, and the parameters within which they were required to make their decision. The judge sequestered the jury during deliberations, which prevented them from learning of the next event to take place during this trial.

THE DEFENDANT IS SHOT

On November 30, 1994, one day after the jury began deliberating his fate, Shakur and Fuller were entering a recording studio shortly after midnight when they were approached by several men with guns. The robbers ordered the men to give them all their jewelry and to lie on the ground. When Shakur reportedly refused, one of the gunmen shot him five times, and the robbers made off with $40,000 worth of jewelry that Shakur had been wearing. The defendant was taken to the hospital, treated and held for observation.

No. 1 with a Bullet: In March 1995, while the rapper was in prison, Shakur's album titled *Me Against the World* was released under the name Two Pac. The record entered the charts at number 1.

Against his doctor's wishes, Shakur left the hospital soon after surgery and, wearing a knit Yankees baseball hat pulled over his bandaged head, returned to the courtroom in a wheelchair. If jury members were startled or curious about the sudden change in the defendant's appearance, Justice Fitzgerald left them to puzzle it out for themselves.

Shakur's courtroom appearance was brief. He was back in the hospital for further treatment when on December 1, the jury returned to the courtroom with its verdict after only three days of deliberation. Shakur and co-defendant Fuller were found guilty of sexual abuse and acquitted on all other charges. Apparently the jury was not convinced that the sodomy or illegal possession of firearms had been proven beyond a reasonable doubt.

Shakur's attorney claimed to be "ecstatic" that the rap star had been acquitted on the more serious charges, but quickly added that the defense would appeal the one guilty verdict. One of the grounds for an appeal was given to the defense several hours before the verdict was reached when Assistant District Attorney James revealed to the court and defense counsel that the prosecution had inadvertently withheld evidence from the defense: photographs of the victim's chest taken the day after the attack had been misfiled and were not found until the morning of the disclosure. While withheld evidence is often sufficient grounds to move for a mistrial, the defense decided to wait until the verdict was announced before determining what action to take. Should the defense decide to appeal the conviction based on the withheld evidence, they would have to show that the evidence was material to the case and that its failure to be included denied the defendant a fair trial.

HIGH DRAMA AT THE SENTENCING

The sentencing took place on February 8, 1995, and it was no less dramatic than the trial. The proceedings began with the victim explaining how the crime had affected her physically, emotionally, and psychologically. "He took advantage of his stardom to abuse me and betray my trust," she declared. Since the attack, she said, she had been turned into the villain while Shakur "has been glorified by his peers and fans."

Shakur stared intently at his accuser while she spoke. When she finished, he stood and, with tears in his eyes, apologized, but it wasn't clear for what. "I'm not apologizing for a crime," he declared. "I hope in time you'll come forth and tell the truth—I am innocent."

Addressing Justice Fitzgerald before sentencing, Shakur virtually accused the judge and the system of racism. "You never looked into my eyes. You never used the wisdom of Solomon. I always felt you had something against me."

Finally, he apologized to the youth of America. "I got so involved in my career that I didn't see this coming. I have no shame, I don't feel shame." This statement received a positive response from the many fans in attendance. At one point, a sheriff had to order a young woman back to her seat after she had leaned over the railing and kissed the rap star on the cheek.

Justice Fitzgerald told Shakur, "This was an act of brutal violence against a helpless woman." And with that he sentenced Shakur to 18-months-to-4$^{1}/_{2}$-half years in prison. Noting that Fuller had no criminal record and that Shakur had been the instigator of the attack, Fitzgerald sentenced Fuller to four months in jail and five years probation.

All the elements found in the lyrics to Shakur's "gangsta rap" songs were present in the trial—violence, sex, guns, and the degradation of a woman. Indeed, his fans won't be shocked or his critics surprised if his next rap hit recites the story of his own trial and jail time.

In spring 1995, Shakur married his long-time fiancée Keisha Morris.

—Penelope Petzold

THE COLIN FERGUSON TRIAL

On December 7, 1993, the daily 5:33 P.M. Long Island Rail Road train left Penn Station in New York City for Hicksville, New York, carrying commuters home. As the train raced into neighboring Nassau County, one of the passengers rose and walked calmly down the aisle, shooting everyone he passed with a 9mm handgun. When the shooter paused to reload, terrified passengers wrestled him down. By then, six people lay dead or dying. Nineteen more were seriously wounded.

The man with the gun was Colin Ferguson, 36, a well-educated, unemployed immigrant from an upper middle-class Jamaican family. His surreal defense would strain debates over mental competency and criminal insanity like few others ever heard in an American courtroom.

Ferguson insisted that he was perfectly sane. In fact, he denied that he was the killer; he claimed that an unidentified white man had done the shooting and then escaped. With a train full of wounded survivors and traumatized onlookers accusing him, Ferguson's claim was clearly either a delusion or a lie.

A court-ordered psychiatric examination determined that Ferguson met both criteria by which defendants are deemed sane enough to stand trial in New York: He understood the nature of the legal proceedings against him and he was able to assist in his own defense. He was also found to have been able to distinguish right from wrong at the time of the shootings.

One month after the shootings, on January 7, 1994, Ferguson was declared mentally competent by Nassau County District Judge Ira Warshawsky. Despite this ruling, Ferguson's court-appointed attorney, Anthony Falanga, said he would still attempt to defend Ferguson on grounds of insanity. Ferguson refused to cooperate with Falanga. After two months of being ignored by his client, Falanga stepped aside when Ferguson agreed to be represented by controversial civil rights attorneys William Kunstler and Ronald Kuby. Ferguson's new lawyers agreed that he was mentally unstable, but they announced that his defense would take a different approach.

When Ferguson was arrested, police found notes in his pockets expressing his hatred of Caucasians, Asians, and "Uncle Tom Negroes." Kunstler and Kuby held that Ferguson's behavior could be tied to a study entitled *Black Rage*. In this 1968 study, psychologists Price Cobbs and William Grier observed that in order to function in society, African Americans suppress feelings of intense anger over racism. Kunstler and Kuby would try to expand this thesis into a "black rage" defense, arguing that continual racist mistreatment was the catalyst that caused Ferguson's delusions and paranoia to explode into violence.

Critics accused the attorneys of manipulating the sensitive state of race relations in New York in order to excuse the acts of a cold-blooded killer. Kunstler and Kuby vowed to press ahead with the "black rage" defense. Their strategy, however, accepted that Ferguson was the killer and that he was mentally unsound. Ferguson rejected both assumptions.

Ferguson then decided to act as his own attorney, against the advice of his lawyers and Nassau County District Judge Donald

During the trial, Ferguson was reprimanded by Judge Belfi for spending too much time doing interviews. The defendant had used the telephone (installed in his jail cell so he could consult his legal advisers) in order to stage a "media blitz," which included calls to the Associated Press, *The Village Voice*, *Larry King Live*, and the *Today* show.

—*The New York Times*, February 15, 1995

Belfi. Because Judge Belfi reaffirmed the mental competency finding on December 9, Ferguson was entitled to represent himself, even though he had no legal training. Furthermore, because the defendant was considered legally sane, Judge Belfi was required to provide the indigent Ferguson with county funds to pay for a private investigator to find "the real killer."

"The trial offers an eerie contrast to O.J. Simpson's. On one coast, an army of high-priced legal talents defends a sane man accused of murder; on the other, a man whose sanity is in serious doubt argues for himself." —*The New York Times*, February 4, 1995

"What we will have now is a complete circus," predicted Kuby.

Although Ferguson dismissed Kunstler and Kuby, he continued to telephone them for advice. Nevertheless Ferguson decided that his only legal advisor in court would be Alton Rose, a Jamaican-born attorney who had known the defendant when he was a young man. Since emotions surrounding the case were so high, Rose made a motion to have the trial moved outside of Nassau County. An appeals court refused, holding that Ferguson, not Rose, would have to make such a request.

Opening statements in the trial began on January 26, 1995, in Mineola, New York. Wearing a bulletproof vest under a handsome suit and speaking evenly, Ferguson said that as the commuter train made its way out of New York City, he had dozed off and someone had stolen his gun and opened fire on the passengers. "Mr. Ferguson was awakened by the gunfire and, amid the confusion, sought to protect himself," Ferguson said, speaking of himself in the third person to an increasingly strange effect in the courtroom. Ferguson told the jury that the charges against him were a racist conspiracy.

Prosecutors produced police photos of victims lying in pools of blood, there were shell casings and bullet holes in the railroad car. Averting his eyes from the pictures, Ferguson objected that the photos were prejudicial in nature, but the judge overruled him.

The pistol wrestled from Ferguson was entered as evidence. As prosecutors passed the weapon back and forth in front of the jury, Ferguson objected when he was not allowed to hold the gun. The judge sent the jury out of the room.

"By not being allowed to hold the weapon, the jurors are given the impression that the court has already made up its mind about my guilt or innocence," Ferguson said. "Therefore, I move for a mistrial."

"This is one of the pitfalls of self-representation," replied Judge Belfi. "No defendant can handle a weapon. You were not singled out. Motion denied."

Survivors of the massacre began to testify. Television viewers across the nation watched incredulously as Ferguson questioned the people he was accused of shooting at point-blank range. Far from appearing terrified, however, most of the victims responded to Ferguson's bizarre queries unflinchingly.

Mary Anne Phillips, the first gunshot victim, testified that she had played dead after she was wounded. Ferguson asked if she kept her eyes closed.

"Yes," replied Phillips, "so you wouldn't come back and shoot me again."

Elizabeth Aviles similarly refused to be intimidated by the man who had shot her in the back. When Ferguson pressed Aviles to describe the gunman, she responded angrily, "I saw you shooting everyone on the train, okay?"

As the trial progressed, the eloquence of Ferguson's frequent objections led many to wonder if he was a crazy man mounting an able defense or a sane man cultivating an appearance of insanity, cynically paving the way for future appeals. He accused the Jewish Defense League of conspiring to kill him and said that the prison murder of cannibal serial killer Jeffrey Dahmer was a rehearsal for his own death behind bars.

Ferguson made a request to subpoena U.S. President Bill Clinton, because the president had personally commended the bravery of George Blum, Michael O'Connor, and Mark McEntee—the three men who subdued the killer at the time of the shootings. The request was denied. Ferguson also argued that the indictment against him contained 93 counts only because the shootings occurred in 1993. "Had it been 1925," Ferguson said, "it would have been 25 counts."

Outside of court, a New York exorcist claimed that the CIA had kidnapped Ferguson and implanted a computer chip in his brain, activating it with an order to kill. Ferguson considered call-

Colin Ferguson being taken to his arraignment from Nassau County Police Headquarters in Mineola, New York, on December 8, 1993. The accused gunman was charged after a rush-hour shooting on the Long Island Railroad commuter train on Tuesday, December 7, 1993. AP/Wide World Photos

ing the exorcist as a witness, but decided against it. Although he was entitled to do so, Ferguson rested his case without calling the defendant he habitually referred to as "Colin Ferguson" to the stand. Carolyn McCarthy, whose husband Dennis had been killed and her son critically wounded in the railroad shootings, described Ferguson as a coward for not taking the stand.

On February 17, the jury considered the case for ten hours. When the jurors returned to court, they acquitted Ferguson on 25 counts of aggravated harassment, but found him guilty of all the other charges, including multiple counts of murder, attempted murder, assault, reckless endangerment, and weapons possession. There had never been any doubt about Ferguson's guilt, said the jury foreman, who explained that the long deliberations concerned the less serious harassment counts.

To attorneys Kunstler and Kuby, Ferguson agreed to pursue an appeal based on grounds that he never should have been found mentally competent to stand trial. To Attorney Rose, however, Ferguson maintained that he was mentally sound. Rose announced that he would not represent Ferguson during any appeals and would ask the state to appoint a public defender to represent his indigent client after sentencing.

On March 21, survivors and family members of the dead filled the court to testify during sentencing recommendations. For two days, people directly touched by the railroad massacre asked Judge Belfi to punish Ferguson severely for the suffering he had inflicted. Robert Giugliano, whom Ferguson had shot in the chest, lunged at the defendant.

"Look at these eyes," shouted Giugliano. "You can't! You're nothing but a piece of garbage!"

When Ferguson accused the wounded of plotting with police against him, victims and their families turned their backs and filed out of the courtroom. Visibly aghast at Ferguson's insensitivity, Attorney Rose asked the judge if he could also leave the room. Judge Belfi denied the request. As Rose sat exasperated beside him, Ferguson declared his innocence in another rambling monologue, which lasted for hours.

"John the Baptist lived in the wilderness, a humble man, and he was put into prison," Ferguson said. "He was beheaded by a criminal justice system similar to this. After his death, we can look back and say with 20-20 hindsight, 'This was a great man.' And as much as I'm hated in Nassau County and America, I believe there are persons that are strengthened by me and my stand."

Judge Belfi saw things differently. "Colin Ferguson, in my almost 21 years on the bench, I have never presided over a trial with a more selfish and self-centered defendant," the judge said before a packed courtroom. "The vicious acts you committed on December 7, 1993, were the acts of a coward."

During the trial the New York State Legislature had re-instituted the death penalty for murder. However, Ferguson would not face execution because his crimes occurred before the law was passed. "Unfortunately, this new law cannot be applied to you," Judge Belfi told Ferguson. "The court is, however, empowered to mete out a sentence which is functionally equivalent to life without parole."

Noting the killer's "total lack of remorse," Judge Belfi sentenced Ferguson to six consecutive 25-years-to-life terms, one for each count of murder. The judge also gave Ferguson 25-year sentences for each of 19 counts of attempted murder—for a total of 475 years. But prison terms for multiple convictions of attempted murder are limited by New York law to a total of 50 years. Thus, Ferguson's combined sentences added up to 200 years. His victims and their families cheered as the sentence was read.

As he was led away, Ferguson called out that he would appeal. Later, as he prepared to make the trip from county jail to a state penitentiary isolation cell, a curious thing happened, which Ferguson's guards attributed to his fear of being killed in prison: Colin Ferguson finally stopped talking.

—Tom Smith

T he case that many people dubbed "the trial of the century" began with the persistent barking and whimpering of a wandering dog at nearly midnight on June 12, 1994. The dog, an Akita found with blood on its paws, led neighbors to the brutally stabbed and slashed bodies of Nicole Brown Simpson and Ronald L. Goldman. Nicole was the ex-wife of football hero and TV spokesman Orenthal James Simpson, known as "O.J." Goldman was a friend of Nicole who worked as a waiter in a restaurant near her home. Both lay in pools of blood on the walkway approaching the entrance of Nicole's condominium at 875 South Bundy Drive in the upscale Brentwood section of Los Angeles, California.

Before dawn, Detectives Philip Vannatter and Tom Lange of the Los Angeles Police Department (LAPD) Robbery-Homicide Division were named lead investigators in the killings and were at the crime scene, which had already been secured by officers from the West Los Angeles station. Ordered by superiors to give Simpson a "personal notification" of his ex-wife's death and arrange care for the Simpsons' two young children, who had been found asleep in Nicole's house and taken to police headquarters, the detectives headed for O.J. Simpson's home. They took along Detective Mark Fuhrman, who had been the first detective to reach the scene. Fuhrman, recalling having been summoned to the house by a 911 domestic violence call made by Nicole Brown Simpson a decade earlier, knew the fastest route through the maze of the fashionable neighborhood.

No one answered the detectives' persistent doorbell-ringing at the locked gates of Simpson's walled estate. While waiting to get in, according to his later testimony, Fuhrman strolled to a Ford Bronco that was parked slightly askew from the curb in the street at the estate's rear gate. He called Vannatter's attention to what appeared to be bloodstains, one just above the driver's outside door handle, others just below that door. Concerned that someone in the house was injured, the lead detective ordered Fuhrman to climb the wall and let the

The murder scene—Nicole Brown Simpson's home at 875 South Bundy in Brentwood.
Courtesy of April Pearce-Lowe

others in. Once they were at the front door, again there was no answer. At a guest house, sleepy-eyed Brian "Kato" Kaelin, who said he was a friend of O.J., referred them to Arnelle Simpson, who also lived in the guest-house complex and was O.J.'s adult daughter by his first wife. When Arnelle let them into the main house, they learned that Simpson had taken a red-eye flight to Chicago at midnight. Detective Ronald Phillips phoned Simpson to tell him the news.

Meantime, Kaelin told Detective Fuhrman that, at about 10:40 the night before, he had heard loud thumps near the air conditioner in the wall of his room—noises so strong they jiggled a picture on his wall. Fuhrman went out and checked a narrow, overgrown passageway between the guest house and the property line's chain-link fence. Returning, he led Phillips to the same rear path and pointed out, lying on the path, a black glove that appeared to be bloody. They agreed that it looked like a mate to a glove they had seen beside Goldman's body. They also observed drops of what looked like blood on the driveway, the path to the front door, and the entryway of the house. The senior detective (according to his later testimony) developed a strong suspicion of Simpson as the killer, declared the Simpson property to be a crime scene, asked that it be secured by crime-scene tape and patrolmen on guard, and obtained a search warrant. The Ford Bronco parked outside the gate was impounded.

When Simpson returned to Los Angeles the next day, Los Angeles police interviewed him for three hours without his lawyer, who said he need not be present. While tape recording a statement from him, Vannatter noticed that the middle finger of Simpson's left hand was bandaged and seemed to be swollen. The detective had the finger photographed, without its bandage, showing two lacerations. Vannatter also had a nurse obtain a sample of Simpson's blood, which the detective then carried to the criminologist on duty investigating the scene at Simpson's home. On Friday morning, June 17, Vannatter told Los Angeles D.A. Gil Garcetti he had probable cause for considering Simpson the prime suspect. The police went to arrest Simpson, but for almost five hours they could not find him.

THE INFAMOUS CHASE

That evening, some 93 million television viewers found their programs interrupted as nearly every station suddenly switched to live coverage from a helicopter above a Los Angeles freeway. Below, long-time Simpson friend Al Cowlings was driving slowly while he reported by cellular phone that O.J. was in the car with a pistol to his own head, intent on suicide. Police cars and ordinary traffic were moving in a leisurely procession behind the Cowlings car—also a white Ford Bronco.

The slow-motion chase lasted 90 minutes. Finally, Cowlings drove into Simpson's driveway at 360 North Rockingham Avenue. At the gate, restrained by police barricades, eager fans waved signs proclaiming "We love the Juice." After an hour of negotiation, the suspect was arrested. On Monday, June 20, the Los Angeles County grand jury charged him with the murders. He was held in jail without bail.

By this time, a media event destined to consume probably more pages of newsprint and hours of broadcast time than any since World War II was well under way. With California courts permitting live TV coverage, Court TV and Cable News Network (CNN) used a single pooled camera to attend every moment of the lengthy preliminary hearing. Talk shows argued each nuance of the reported evidence. Supermarket tabloids sold out, increased print runs, sold out again, paid lavishly for supposedly authentic accounts from presumably knowledgeable experts and genuine potential witnesses. Hollywood tour buses established new routes along Rockingham and Bundy. Gawking motorists clogged Brentwood's usually quiet lanes. The frenzied media and sightseeing circus seemed to forget that two people had been murdered.

The mug shot of O. J. Simpson, taken June 17, 1994, soon after he surrendered to police at his Brentwood estate in Los Angeles, California. Simpson was charged with two counts of murder in connection with the killings of his ex-wife, Nicole, and her friend, Ronald Goldman. AP/Wide World Photos

But Simpson faced that reality when Judge Kathleen Kennedy-Powell ruled that there was enough evidence for him to stand trial for the double murder. At his arraignment on Friday, July 29, 1994, his attorney, Robert L. Shapiro, a well-known West Coast lawyer whom many considered a master legal tactician, was joined by America's perhaps best-known African-American trial lawyer, Johnnie L. Cochran, Jr., who had tried 31 murder cases and had recently represented singer Michael Jackson in his out-of-court settlement against charges of child molestation. Breaking court practice that says the accused may plead only the simple words "guilty" or "not guilty," Simpson firmly declared that he was "absolutely, 100 percent not guilty."

Prosecutor Marcia Clark, a 40-year-old Deputy District Attorney, was tackling her 21st murder prosecution in 13 years in the D.A.'s office and had not lost a murder case in 10 years.

Considered rock-solid tough by courthouse buffs, she was a recognized expert in trials involving circumstantial evidence and testing for DNA—deoxyribonucleic acid, a complex molecule that makes up the chromosomes of every living cell and provides a blueprint for all inherited traits. DNA analysis of blood and other evidence was expected to be a major factor in the outcome of the trial.

At Clark's right hand was Deputy District Attorney Christopher A. Darden, an African-American prosecutor widely experienced in murder trials. Co-counsel with Clark was William Hodgman, an expert at pulling complex facts together into comprehensible evidence of guilt who had successfully convicted Charles Keating, Jr., in the complicated Lincoln Savings Bank swindling case.

O.J. Simpson's home on Rockingham in Brentwood, cordoned off to prevent sightseers from getting too close. The nation's first real and most memorable view of Simpson's home was from the aerial shots, from helicopter cameras, as much of the nation watched the now-infamous chase of the white Ford Bronco aired live on TV. That chase ended just inside the gate of Simpson's home. Courtesy of April Pearce-Lowe

Simpson sought a speedy trial. Defense and prosecuting attorneys worked around the clock to prepare their cases. In October, Judge Lance A. Ito started interviewing 304 prospective jurors, each of whom had to fill out a 75-page questionnaire. November 3 found 12 jurors seated: Eight blacks, one white, two Hispanics, and one who described himself as half American Indian and half white.

Their ages ranged from 22 to 52. Eight were women. On December 8, Judge Ito seated 12 alternates, including seven blacks, four whites, and one Hispanic. They ranged in age from 24 to 72. Nine were women.

Syndicated columnist Joel Achenbach, wrote in "Why Things Are" on April 9, 1995, that Ito is "time-obsessed. He's put a clock on every wall. . . . He had three hourglasses next to him at the start of the trial. . . . At last count he had seven." After further explaining that the judge likes gadgets and tools, Achenbach, in one of many irreverent jabs the trial and its players were taking at the time, encouraged his readers to "spread the rumor that Ito is wearing pajamas under his robe."

During December and January, in a continual round of hearings and debates punctuated by internal feuds among the defense lawyers and squabbling between prosecution and defense, Judge Ito turned down defense requests to cancel hearings on the admissibility of DNA evidence, arbitrated wrangling over whether the prosecution might present evidence on domestic violence in the Simpson marriage, and ordered the jury sequestered. Meantime, eager buyers welcomed the publication of Simpson's book *I Want to Tell You* and of a Faye Resnick book purportedly telling all she knew about the Simpsons' relationship.

THE TRIAL OF THE CENTURY BEGINS

The trial itself began on Monday, January 24, 1995. In her opening statement, chief prosecutor Marcia Clark assured the jury they would learn about a trail of blood that led from the death scene on South Bundy to a pair of socks in O.J.'s own bedroom on Rockingham. The path of "blood where there should be no blood" would be proved by DNA testing. Prosecutor Darden added a description of the defendant's years of abusive behavior toward his wife–his obsession to control her, his violent jealousy. "If he couldn't have her," said Darden, "he didn't want anybody else to have her." Clark warned the jury to be "ever vigilant" against the defense lawyers, who, she said, would raise bogus doubts at every opportunity. "You will be tested and tempted throughout this case," she said, "to accept the unreasonable and be distracted by the irrelevant."

Cochran's opening for the defense brought Simpson across the courtroom to the jury box to exhibit his scarred left knee as confirmation that he was so disabled he couldn't commit murder. Next came a surprise: The defense would introduce more than a dozen witnesses they had not yet revealed to the prosecution. This failure to notify the prosecution was a tactic so "disgusting and appalling," raged Clark, that it was "trial by ambush." The news sent prosecutor Hodgman to the hospital with chest pains.

Within days, lawyers and lay persons alike saw an emerging pattern: Continual and countless interruptions with objections from each side of the courtroom, one "sidebar" conference after another with the judge beyond earshot of the jury, special hearings while the jury languished in their waiting room, a judge intolerant of the media but overly tolerant of the many lawyers on each side and slow to settle their endless disagreements.

Before formal testimony began, Judge Ito broke precedent by allowing prosecutor Clark to amend her opening statement–a feat never before permitted in a California criminal case. She told the jury that one of the defense's newly-disclosed witnesses, whom the defense expected to testify to seeing four men near the murder scene, was "a known liar and a Simpson case groupie" who was "one of those people who comes [sic] out of the woodwork in high-profile cases so they can get involved."

The prosecution set out first to establish Simpson's cruel and abusive treatment of Nicole throughout their marriage. The jury heard Nicole's screams on the tape of a 911 call at 3:58 A.M. on January 1, 1989, and saw Polaroid photos, taken by the police, of her battered face that night. As a result, they learned, Simpson had been charged with spousal battering; he pleaded no contest, paid a $750 fine, and was required to undergo counseling. They also heard 14 minutes of 911 tape from October 1993 during which he screamed obscenities at his wife.

Simpson's longtime friend, former police officer Ronald G. Shipp, testified that on June 13—the evening after the killings—Simpson told him, "To be honest, Shipp, I've had some dreams about killing her." Cross-examination tried to blame Shipp's testimony on his known drinking problems and to discredit his supposed friendship. But the cross-examination backfired when Shipp disclosed that he had not mentioned Simpson's dreams because he had concluded that Simpson was the murderer and "I didn't want to be going down as being the person to nail O.J."

In tearfully emotional testimony, Nicole's sister Denise told how, in the late 1980s, she saw Simpson pick up his wife and hurl her against a wall, then throw her physically out of their house. Her testimony was punctuated by a barrage of defense objections and sidebar conferences with the judge.

Then the prosecution turned to the events of June 12, 1994. Karen Lee Crawford, who was manager of the Mezzaluna restaurant that Sunday night, recounted how Mrs. Simpson's mother called at 9:37 P.M. about her daughter's lost eyeglasses, how she found them and put them in a white envelope, how waiter Ron Goldman departed at about 9:50 on the 10-minute walk to drop them off at Nicole's house. Nicole's neighbor, Pablo Fenives, told of hearing the "very distinctive barking" and "plaintive wail" of a dog at 10 to 15 minutes into the 10 o'clock news. Neighbor Eva Stein testified that "very loud, very persistent" barking awakened her at about 10:15 and kept her from getting back to sleep. Neighbor Steven Schwab pinpointed walking his own dog at 10:30, encountering a wandering and agitated Akita dog trailing its leash and with bloody paws that he examined but found uninjured. His neighbor Sukru Boztepe described taking the bloodied dog for a calming walk only to find it "getting more nervous and pulling me harder" as they neared Nicole's home, where "I saw a lady laying down, full of blood." He banged on neighborhood doors trying to call the police, then flagged down a squad car.

Now, as Robert Riske, the squad car cop, described what he found, the jury saw photographs that Judge Ito did not release to the press or for broadcast: "We observed a female white in a black dress," said Riske, "laying in a puddle on the walkway," her blood flowing along the walkway grouting and across the terrazzo tiles. Then he saw Goldman's body nearby and touched his eyeball "basically to verify that he was dead." The photos displayed in the courtroom brought the jury forward in their chairs and sent Nicole Brown Simpson's mother and father out of the room. Riske described seeing a white envelope (later proved to contain the eyeglasses from the restaurant), Goldman's beeper, a black glove, and a blue knit ski cap on the ground near the bodies. He told of finding young Sydney and Justin, the Simpsons' children, asleep and escorting them from the rear of the house.

On Sunday, February 12, 1995, a long motorcade invaded the Brentwood section. It brought judge, jurors, prosecutors, and defense lawyers to a two-hour inspection of the Bundy crime scene, then a three-hour tour of the Rockingham estate–preceded by drive-by visits to Goldman's apartment and the Mezzaluna restaurant. Simpson, not wearing handcuffs. waited outside the Bundy house in an unmarked police car but entered his Rockingham home.

By now, the "trial of the century" was setting new records. Cyberspace was awash in trial information as the commercial network services vied to provide the most extensive coverage. Compuserve's 2.6 million customers, Prodigy's 1.2 million, America Online's 1.5 million–all could download as many as 20,000 messages related to the case. Some 98 of the 100 highest-rated basic cablevision programs in the first quarter of 1994 were Simpson-related. From Manhattan to Taiwan, no man (or woman) was an island uninformed.

When police sergeant David Rossi testified, famed attorney F. Lee Bailey, part of the all-star Simpson defense team, cross-examined for the defense. In a fiery display of bluster, disdain, and sarcasm, he tried to prove that a horde of witless cops had traipsed over vital and perhaps invisible evidence, neglected to call the coroner promptly, and generally ignored the "cardinal rules" of law enforcement.

Detective Ron Phillips recounted his call to Simpson in Chicago. The defendant, he said, seemed upset at the news of his ex-wife's death but oddly unconcerned about how she died. Detective Tom Lange testified that Nicole Simpson was probably killed first, because the bottoms of her bare feet were clean. "The victim was more than likely struck before there was any blood that flowed," he said–a key point in the prosecution's theory that Simpson set out to kill his former wife whereas Goldman inadvertently stumbled upon the scene.

ROSA LOPEZ TAKES THE STAND

Thursday, February 24, brought a daylong hearing over whether defense lawyers might question Rosa Lopez, a Spanish-speaking maid who worked next door to Simpson, out of sequence and on videotape rather than in the jury's hearing. Lopez was

threatening to leave the United States to return to El Salvador. Judge Ito permitted the testimony, in which she said through a translator that she saw the Simpson Bronco parked on the street the night of the murders, but her credibility came under severe question when the prosecution proved she was wrong in claiming she had booked a flight to El Salvador for the following Saturday, had been fired from her job, had no other travel plans, and had been given a ticket (for which the defense had paid) to Los Angeles from another city (where she was hiding) by her niece. To many questions, her simple responses were "I don't remember" or "If you say so."

The Lopez testimony ended with Judge Ito fining two of Simpson's lawyers—Johnnie L. Cochran and Carl Douglas—$950 each for failing to give prosecutors a recording, made some six months earlier, of their chief investigator's interview with Lopez. The judge stopped just short of reporting the lawyers to the California bar.

Cross-examining Detective Lange, Cochran proposed two hypotheses for what happened at the murder scene. In one, he suggested that drug dealers had encountered Mrs. Simpson while attempting to kill her friend and house guest, Faye Resnick, an admitted cocaine abuser. In the other, he suggested that "an assassin or assassins" had followed Goldman to South Bundy. The detective responded, "I had absolutely no other evidence that would point me in any other direction" than Simpson.

> "She [Rosa Lopez] smokes their whole case. They're betting on a dog. We're betting on Rosa." —O.J. Simpson defense attorney F. Lee Bailey, on *Larry King Live,* Friday, March 3, 1995

March 1 saw the replay of what was becoming a frequent scene: the removal of a juror, the fourth to be asked to leave. The panel of alternates now stood at eight.

DETECTIVE FUHRMAN IS GRILLED BY THE DEFENSE

Detective Mark Fuhrman took the stand. Anticipating the defense's plan to depict him as a racist, the prosecution presented

The trial in session on Friday, February 17, 1995: Prosecutor Marcia Clark returns a bloody glove, a key piece of prosecution evidence found near Nicole Brown Simpson's home, to a plastic bag. Los Angeles Police Detective Tom Lange, one of the lead police investigators of the double murder, is shown on the stand (at left).

the jury with a good-looking and athletic cop who could keep his cool and who had neither the inclination to plant the glove at Rockingham–nor the opportunity. Defense attorney F. Lee Bailey grilled him aggressively on the time he spent behind the Rockingham house, on whether he had a financial stake in the case, on why he had hired a lawyer, and on whether he had made racist statements in 1985. Despite Bailey's dramatic gesticulations and insistent innuendo, the detective remained calm and polite, his composure unshaken.

St. Patrick's Day brought a fake bomb scare that emptied the courthouse temporarily. Judge Ito sent another juror home, purportedly for violating orders by surreptitiously writing a book. Detective Vannatter testified on how the cut on Simpson's finger raised his suspicions, and defense attorney Shapiro argued that Vannatter, in obtaining a search warrant, had misrepresented that Simpson had taken an unexpected trip to Chicago and that blood on the Bronco was human when that had not been proved.

HOUSE GUEST KATO KAELIN TESTIFIES

Shaggy-haired Brian "Kato" Kaelin was next. He testified that Simpson told him how, on the evening of the murders, his ex-wife tried to keep him from speaking with their daughter after her dance recital and that he complained about the tight dress Mrs. Simpson was wearing. He described driving with Simpson to a McDonald's and said he did not know the defendant's whereabouts between their return at 9:35 and 11:00 when he helped load Simpson into the limo. The defendant did not appear to be at home, he said, when the limo driver arrived, as he, Kato, had to let the car in. He also described hearing the thumps on his bedroom wall, and he related how he offered to cross the driveway and pick up Simpson's knapsack (which was last seen that evening) but the defendant said, "I'll get it."

Kaelin's testimony hovered between elusive and evasive to the point that Judge Ito granted prosecutor Clark's request that the actor be designated a hostile witness. A typical Kaelin response was this one during cross-examination by defense attorney Shapiro: "I'm an actor, so, the more of a—no, it was sort of, 'they can't be wearing those tight outfits,' but it wasn't a degree of upset, it's such a hard thing to—being upset, it wasn't throwing things, it wasn't wearing that mini-skirt, it wasn't like that—tough question."

Limousine driver Allan Park testified on his arrival at 10:22 for the appointment to drive Simpson to the airport, his inability to rouse anyone to open the Rockingham gate until after he had seen a tall black man hurry into the unlit house, his loading the car and later Simpson's turning Kaelin away from the small black bag by saying, "No, no. That's O.K. I'll get it, I'll get it."

O.J. Simpson's neighbor, Charles Cale, who walked his dog down Rockingham between 9:30 and 9:45 P.M. on June 12, testified that he saw no Bronco at that time. He was followed by criminologist Dennis Fung, who described the gathering of physical evidence—the pair of leather gloves, the knit cap, footprints, hair samples, and blood drops—while 10 defense attorneys listened.

Meantime, the trial bumped to one of its frequent halts as Judge Ito ordered a sixth juror to step down because she had failed to reveal that she had been a victim of domestic abuse. She promptly predicted a hung jury, said that jurors had broken the judge's rules by discussing the case among themselves and with others in unmonitored phone calls, and accused a white juror of kicking and stepping on black jurors. The judge subpoenaed her for a hearing in his chambers, and said afterward that she should not be taken seriously. He also listened to defense allegations that the prosecution had tailed and spied on defense witnesses and experts.

Now Fung faced a long, intensive cross-examination by defense attorney Barry Scheck, a New York lawyer considered an expert on blood-related evidence. He concentrated on denigrating the work of Fung's associate, Andrea Mazzola, as that of a novice who had worked at fewer than a handful of crime scenes. Scheck seemed determined to accuse Fung of covering for detectives Vannatter, Lange, and Fuhrman because he feared for his job. Implying that Fung was an inept and deceitful witness, Scheck cited errors and inconsistencies in note-taking, in leaving blood samples in a hot truck for hours, and in not conducting tests on bloodstains that Fuhrman said he had pointed out on the Bronco but later filing false reports about them. The Scheck cross-examination clearly established the defense's determination to prove that the LAPD was staffed with incompetents and liars who conspired to frame the defendant.

As Fung stepped down after nine intensive days on the witness stand, the jury saw him receive hearty handshakes from Simpson, Scheck, and Cochran, and an embrace from Shapiro, who, the day before, had apologized for handing out fortune cookies from a restaurant called Hang Fung.

Now Judge Ito excused a sixth juror. She told him, "I just can't take it anymore." Andrea Mazzola, LAPD evidence collector who had assisted criminologist Fung, demonstrated how easy it was to pick up exhibits despite inexperience. And suddenly the trial took its strangest turn yet: Thirteen of the jurors and alternates, refusing to leave their hotel, demanded that Judge Ito talk with them. When he said he would do so only in court, each arrived in the courtroom dressed entirely in black. Their complaint? The judge, responding to assertions that sheriff's deputies assigned to guard jurors had sown racial discord among them, had replaced three deputies. Testimony was suspended for two days while the judge calmed the protesters by meeting with them individually. Following this hiatus, observers noticed a "new" Judge Ito who cut the lunch hour by one-third, ordered spectators removed for whispering, and warned the lawyers against lengthy objections as well as motions made during jury time.

May came. The judge dismissed a seventh juror, a 25-year-old black flight attendant, replacing her with a 28-year-old Hispanic woman. Five alternates remained.

THE SCIENTIFIC EVIDENCE IS PRESENTED

Now began the presentation of the first scientific evidence that could link the defendant to the crime. LAPD forensic chemist Gregory Matheson testified that a blood drop found on the Bundy walkway could not have come from 99.5 percent of the people in Los Angeles but could be Simpson's, that blood found on socks in Simpson's bedroom could have come from Mrs. Simpson but not from the defendant. Cross-examining, defense attorney Robert Blasier repeated a litany now familiar to the jury and to trial-followers around the world: Police custody of blood samples was incompetent, the victims' bodies were wrongly covered with improper blankets, the cops were late in arriving at the crime scene, laboratory tweezers were not cleaned properly, blood evidence was contaminated by storage in a hot truck, 1.5 millimeters of Simpson's blood sample mysteriously disappeared.

Presentation of DNA evidence began as Robin Cotton, director of Cellmark Diagnostics in Germantown, Maryland, gave jurors a crash course in molecular biology, then linked Simpson to the crime scene by testifying that DNA tests revealed a genetic match between the defendant and blood stains found near the victims, thus bolstering the prosecution argument that Simpson cut himself while committing the murders. After five days of testimony, Cotton was cross-examined by defense attorney Peter Neufeld, who questioned her estimate that only one in 170 million African-Americans and Caucasians showed the same genetic pattern as Simpson. In probability statistics, she replied, the numbers "mean what they mean, they don't mean anything else." Neufeld pushed on until she said, "A number isn't an opinion." Meantime, exasperated by the contentious behavior of Neufeld as well as prosecutor George Clarke, Judge Ito fined each $250, payable on the spot.

Gary Sims, lead forensic analyst at the California Justice Department's DNA laboratory, testified that blood on the glove found at Rockingham matched Goldman's blood, and that the socks found in Simpson's bedroom with his ex-wife's blood on them probably were being worn when they were splattered. Blood stains in the Bronco, he testified, showed the genetic patterns of both victims and the defendant. In addition, he said, tests on the glove's blood, in terms of probability, put Simpson's gene type at one in 41 billion blacks. Finally, under cross-examination, Sims minimalized the possibility of cross-contamination of blood samples—that is, one being tainted by another—in the laboratory.

May 24 brought to the stand Collin Yamauchi, LAPD criminal investigator who processed DNA studies of blood from the crime. Prosecutor Rockne Harmon, following the prosecution strategy of heading off defense claims of "examination bias," asked him if what he had seen in the media had led to such bias. To the dismay of the prosecutors, the witness replied, "I heard on the news that he's got an airtight alibi—he's in Chicago." The defense team leapt to its feet and the judge ordered the jury out of the room as the defense argued that Yamauchi apparently was privy to the tape-recorded statement that Simpson had made to the police on June 14. As a result of Yamauchi's reply, the defense insisted, the jury should be allowed to hear Simpson's statement—a move that would give the defense the advantage of exposing the jury to Simpson's account of events without subjecting him to cross-examination. The judge, noting that Yamauchi had referred only to second-hand stories in the press, rebuffed the motion.

The pool of alternate jurors shrank again as Judge Ito dismissed a juror whom a juror dismissed earlier had accused of kicking her and of hitting an elderly juror on the head. Like all dismissed jurors, this one immediately talked with the press and declared, "They would need a lot more evidence to convince me."

An evidentiary issue bitterly fought by the defense was settled in favor of the prosecution when Judge Ito decided to allow the jury to see more than three dozen extremely graphic photographs of the bodies of the victims. The pictures came with the testimony of Dr. Lakshmanan Sathyavagiswaran, chief medical examiner of Los Angeles County. Prosecutor Brian Kelberg, anticipating defense tactics, immediately produced an acknowledgment from the doctor that his deputy medical examiner, Irwin Golden, had made mistakes in performing the autopsies on the bodies of the victims.

Two more jurors were ousted "for good cause," reducing the alternates' pool to two. Meantime, a member of the Los Angeles Board of Supervisors estimated the cost of the trial through the end of May at $4,986,167 and growing at a rate of $1 million each month.

Dr. Sathyavagiswaran demonstrated how Mrs. Simpson faced her killer's slashing knife and absorbed a severe blow to the head that probably knocked her out. Goldman was then killed, he surmised, before the killer slashed Mrs. Simpson's throat while she lay on the ground. During the initial bloody testimony, Simpson was observed to be distressed, breathing deeply, grinding his teeth, and resting his head on one hand with his eyes closed. Next day, as the disturbing testimony continued, he seemed to have regained his self-control. When the bloody descriptions forced one juror to ask to leave the courtroom, however, the judge cut short "a long day." Next day, the coroner detailed how Goldman was stabbed and slashed more than two dozen times before he died. As to the time of the deaths—a question raised frequently by the defense—Dr. Sathyavagiswaran told the prosector he could estimate, based solely on the scientific evidence, that they occurred between 9:00 P.M. and 12:45 A.M., and said no pathologist could be expected to give a more exact time.

Before the doctor's cross-examination, the prosecution announced that it would not call Dr. Golden, whose many mistakes were admitted but considered unimportant by his supervisor, as a witness. The defense immediately said it would call Golden as its own witness.

Cross-examination of the coroner, after his nine days on direct, was brief. Defense attorney Shapiro seemed to sense that his questions had been preempted by the prosecution's careful exposure of the coroner's awareness of errors committed by his assistant.

THE GLOVES AND THE SHOEPRINTS

Yet another dramatic moment was launched by the testimony of Brenda Vemich, a merchandise buyer who specialized in gloves for the Bloomingdale's department store in New York City. After she identified the expensive brand and size—extra large—of the bloody gloves, prosecutor Darden asked the defendant to put them on. Wearing latex gloves (to protect the evidence), Simpson laboriously pulled and squeezed, while straining and grimacing, to get the leather gloves on. Finally he held up both hands with the obviously too-tight gloves partway on. Critics declared a major prosecution blunder. Defense attorney Cochran, always ready to talk to the press as he arrived and departed from the courthouse, declared the trial as good as over because, he said, of four words: "The gloves don't fit."

F.B.I. agent William J. Bodziak, an expert on shoe prints, testified that the bloody honey-combed print found at the crime scene was not in the F.B.I.'s vast files but had been traced to a $160-a-pair Italian designer brand, Bruno Magli. They were size 12—Simpson's size—of which only 299 pairs had been distributed in the United States. When cross-examiner F. Lee Bailey proposed that two professional assassins had left the imprints of the designer shoes, the witness bluntly replied, "Ridiculous."

Now the prosecution called Richard Rubin, an experienced glove salesman and former executive of the glove manufacturer, Aris Isotoner. He testified that the expensive leather gloves were subject to 15 percent shrinkage from exposure to moisture. Prosecutor Darden presented the defendant with a brand-new pair of the same gloves in size extra-large, flown directly from its Philippine manufacturer. Simpson, this time not wearing latex gloves, easily put them on. Rubin declared them a perfect fit.

The scene produced such contentious jockeying between prosecutor Darden and defense attorney Cochran that Judge Ito fined each $250. "For Johnnie, that's like a bar tab," commented Darden. The judge later reduced the fine to $100.

The next witness, Airtouch Cellular's custodian of records Luelen Robertson, testified briefly that Simpson used his cellular phone to speak with his ex-wife on June 12 and to try unsuccessfully to reach his current girlfriend, Paula Barbieri, as late as 10:03 that evening. Another witness, a lawyer for the Mirage Hotel in Las Vegas, testified on the girlfriend's whereabouts at the time.

The prosecution introduced Dr. Bruce Weir, an internationally known expert on statistics and genetics, to testify on the probability of two or three unknown persons having contributed to the blood evidence. On cross-examination, he conceded that he had failed to include a genetic marker found in Simpson's blood, thus overstating the probability that his blood was in the Bronco and on the Rockingham glove. Pressed by defense attorney Neufeld, he denied shading his findings to help the prosecution. "When I do calculations," he said testily, "I do not consider forensic implications, and if you're suggesting that I do I will disabuse you of that right now."

Neufeld pressed on until Judge Ito cut him off. "Mr. Neufeld," he said, "this is the same question you have now asked for the eighth time." Shortly, the judge fined Neufeld $250 for his loudness during a bench conference.

Next day, Dr. Weir—his arrogance reduced—provided revised findings, reducing the chance of two unknown people contributing to the blood on the Bronco steering wheel from 1 in 59 to 1 in 26, and, on the Rockingham glove, from 1 in 3,900 to 1 in 1,600.

Denise Lewis, laboratory technician for the LAPD, and Susan Brockbank, LAPD criminal evidence expert, testified on their handling of hair and trace evidence—blond and dark human hairs and animal hairs found on the dark blue knit cap left near the bodies of Goldman and Mrs. Simpson, as well as hairs found on the bloody gloves. Robert Blasier's cross-examination renewed the defense's determination to prove that evidence was handled sloppily, as Lewis disclosed that clothing and other items were labeled and stored haphazardly by the coroner's office.

The following day, Ito decided that because the prosecution had bungled the disclosure of a report by witness Douglas Deedrick, unit chief of the FBI's hair and fiber section, the witness would not be allowed to disclose that fibers found on the knit cap and the Bundy glove could have come only from a few Broncos—including Simpson's—built in late 1993 and 1994. Observers noted the judge's outrage and his quick and decisive action over the prosecution blunder.

Deedrick testified that his study of the knit cap revealed 12 hairs that matched those of O.J. Simpson. A ruling by the judge in favor of the defense, however, prevented Deedrick from using the word "match" in describing hairs taken from Goldman's shirt and from the Bundy glove. He said they "resembled" Simpson's hair. Prosecutor Clark produced testimony that the Bundy glove, which had only one of Mrs. Simpson's hairs, probably fell off the murderer's hand early in the crime, whereas the Rockingham glove stayed on and picked up four of Mrs. Simpson's hairs, several of Goldman's, and others that might have come from the Akita dog.

Turning to fibers, the FBI witness said that the Rockingham glove and the knit cap found at Bundy both carried extremely unusual carpet fibers. Three different high-powered microscopes, he said, revealed "three-lobe nylon fibers with knobs at the end of each lobe" that resembled a child's set of jacks. In examining thousands of samples over years, he added, he had never seen anything like them. They matched the carpet of Simpson's Bronco.

Ending four days of testimony, Deedrick again said Simpson had "very distinctive hairs" like those found in Goldman's shirt and on the knit cap, Prosecutor Clark then read into the record a statement from Mrs. Simpson's mother reviewing the family attendance at the June 12 dance recital, the Mezzaluna dinner afterward, and the phone call to retrieve the lost eyeglasses. With that, Clark announced, "The people rest."

It was Thursday, July 6, 1995. Twenty-four weeks and 92 days of prosecution testimony had gone by. Some 34,500 pages of transcript had recorded the words of 58 witnesses and their interrogators, as well as the presentation of 488 exhibits. The judge dismissed the jury until the following Monday, when, he said, "we will proceed with the presentation of the defense case."

THE DEFENSE MAKES ITS CASE

The defense of O. J. Simpson began on Monday morning, July 10, 1995. The first defense witnesses were Simpson family members who had spent the evening of June 13, 1994, with him. Simpson's sister, Carmelita Durio, and his eldest daughter, Arnelle, said he was "distraught" when informed of the murders. Then came his 73-year-old mother, Eunice. "He seemed very upset," she testified. "Shocked." She also gave television viewers, after more than a year of hearing lawyers, cops, and commentators pronounce the defendant's first name "OR-en-thall," the chance to learn that his mother called him "o-REN-thal."

Next day, Jack McKay, an executive who had drawn Simpson as a golf partner at a celebrity tournament four days before the slayings said the defendant was especially cordial for a celebrity and was eager to pose for photographs. Cross-examining, Marcia Clark brought out that the Hertz Corporation, for which Simpson was a spokesman, had been paying the defendant for his affability.

The defense called Danny Mandel and Ellen Aaronson. On Sunday evening, June 12, they said, they walked through the Bundy neighborhood to the Mezzaluna restaurant. Strolling back at about 10:25 P.M., they passed 875 South Bundy and neither saw nor heard anything unusual.

Denise Pilnak, a South Bundy neighbor, saying she was "a stickler for time," showed the jury she wore two watches on her left wrist. The neighborhood was "exceptionally quiet," she said, when she heard a dog bark at about 10:33 to 10:35. On cross-examination, she admitted giving various other times in police statements and interviews with the press.

Wednesday, July 12, brought defense witness Robert Heidstra, who testified that as he walked his dog on Bundy at about 10:40 P.M. he heard two persons arguing. One shouted "Hey! Hey! Hey!" Then came the frenzied wailing of a dog. Next, a white sport utility vehicle sped south. Cross-examination disclosed that Heidstra had told friends the voices were a younger white man's and an older black man's, and that Simpson's was one.

Johnnie Cochran objected furiously. Judge Ito sent the jury out. "You can't tell by someone's voice when they're black," said the seething Cochran. "That's racist, and I resent it."

Speaking directly to Cochran rather than to the court—an attitude forbidden in courtroom protocol and one the judge had frequently warned against—Darden said, "If the statement is racist, then he is the racist, not me, O.K.?"

"I didn't say you," said Cochran.

"That's what you're suggesting," replied Darden.

Judge Ito stood up. "I'm so mad at both of you, I'm about to hold both of you in contempt." He declared a recess and headed off the bench.

"I apologize, Your Honor," said Darden.

The judge tossed his response over his shoulder. "It will take more than that."

Later, Darden asked the witness whether a driver could get from Bundy to Simpson's home in four minutes. "If he's speeding, yes," said Heidstra.

Witness Wayne Stanfield, the American Airlines pilot on Simpson's red-eye flight, told of asking his celebrity passenger at 2:45 A.M. to sign his logbook. He said he had seen no cuts on Simpson's left hand. A courier who obtained a Simpson autograph at the Los Angeles airport earlier that evening agreed. Cross-examined, both men admitted they had hardly been looking for such cuts.

Several Hertz employees and passengers on Simpson's flights testified that they had seen no cuts on his fingers. One passenger, copyright lawyer Mark Partridge, said Simpson told him that he had just learned of the murders. Unfazed, Partridge (who copyrighted his own eight-page statement after the trip) asked for and received a Simpson autograph.

Dr. Robert Huizenga, former team physician for the Los Angeles Raiders, cited a litany of ailments he found while examining the defendant within days after the murders. They included two kinds of arthritis and "a whole array of the typical post-NFL injury syndromes," all of which meant that, for Simpson, "fast walking, slow jogging would be difficult if not impossible."

Deputy District Attorney Brian Kelberg cross-examined. Had the doctor wondered whether Simpson "had a motive to lie regarding his symptoms?" The team doctor said he had considered that, because potential draft choices often lied to avoid disclosing their ailments.

The prosecutors introduced a Simpson exercise video made only two weeks before the murders. Kelberg argued that Simpson's football experience left him well equipped to "play through pain," benefiting from an "adrenaline rush" that could have carried him through the intense physical stress of committing the murders. The doctor agreed.

A 45-minute videotaped workout was shown with the jury absent. In one out-take, Simpson and a trainer threw punches in the air. "You got to get your space in if you're working out with your wife, if you know what I mean," the taped Simpson said. "You can always blame it on working out." The remark, said Kelberg in arguing for court permission to show the tape, proved "that he beats his wife or thinks beating a wife is of no consequence." The judge admitted the tape because its probative value was "substantial."

Simpson's barber testified that the defendant never dyed his hair (some hairs found on the knit cap were dyed) and had dandruff in the warm months (the knit cap showed no dandruff). To demonstrate the prosecution's "rush to judgment," Cochran produced the police officer who had handcuffed Simpson when he got out of his car after the low-speed freeway chase. On cross-examination, the officer said he had never seen a murder suspect handled so gently.

The next two witnesses proved to be embarrassments for the defense. Tow-truck driver John Meraz said he saw no bloodstains when he hauled the Bronco to a holding yard. Marcia Clark's cross-examination showed photos of the stains taken before the towing and impeached Meraz's credibility by revealing that he had stolen (but later returned) receipts from the car.

Even more devastating to the defense was the testimony of fitness instructor Richard Walsh. Cross-examined, he said Simpson's stamina had been remarkable through the 12-hour taping of the fitness video and that three minutes of strenuous exertion gave him no difficulty.

Willie Ford, an LAPD cameraman, testified that he saw no socks when he videotaped Simpson's bedroom at 4:13 P.M. on June 13 as a precaution against possible lawsuits charging damage or theft during the police search. On cross-examination, Ford admitted he had videotaped the room only after it had been searched. Detective Adelberto Luper said he saw the socks on the floor earlier, at 12:30 P.M.

Josephine "Gigi" Guarin, the live-in maid at Rockingham, told of Simpson's meticulous habits, including folding dirty clothes, and said he did not leave socks lying around. Cross-examining, Darden suggested that the defendant's unusual lack of tidiness—socks on the bedroom floor, a towel on the bathroom floor—proved frantic behavior that night.

Turning to scientific evidence to support its theory of a police conspiracy to frame Simpson, the defense called on Fredric Rieders, Ph.D., to interpret FBI tests of blood on the socks and on the rear gate at Bundy. The Vienna-born forensic toxicologist, who brought a professorial air of condescension to the witness stand, said both blood specimens contained EDTA, a chemical used in test tubes to prevent coagulation of blood.

Defense witness Roger Martz, chief of the FBI's chemistry toxicology unit, disagreed. "Everyone is saying I found EDTA, but I am not saying that," he testified. "Those blood stains did not come from preserved blood." Rieders, he said, had jumped to a conclusion.

Cross-examined, Martz said he had found EDTA in his own blood in the same trace amounts as on the evidence, for the compound was a preservative in many foods. "It's only logical to assume that if a person is eating EDTA," he said, "some of it will be in their blood."

Prosecutor Clark drew from Martz a clear distinction between "indications of" EDTA (meaning *it might* be EDTA) and "identification of" EDTA (meaning *it is* EDTA). "There are 11 million chemicals in the world," he said, "so you must be sure before you say you've identified a chemical."

Herbert MacDonnell, a member of the International Association of Blood Stain Pattern Analysts, who had supervised 43 "bloodstain institutes," testified that blood found on the sock in Simpson's bedroom got there not by spattering, as prosecution testimony had held, but by smearing.

On Friday, July 28, Johnnie Cochran was in North Carolina asking the Superior Court to order a screenwriter to testify on Mark Fuhrman's use of racial slurs. The judge ruled that the writer's conversations with Fuhrman, which were recorded as research for a screenplay, were immaterial to the murder trial.

The defense brought in testimony from police nurse Thano Peratis who drew Simpson's blood into a tube containing EDTA preservative on June 13. He said he obtained between 7.9 and 8.1 milliliters of blood. The defense continued to insist that 1.5 milliliters were missing.

John Gerdes, a molecular biologist, testified that the LAPD laboratory had a "chronic" and "substantial" problem with contamination. "Worse than any other laboratory you've ever seen?" asked defense lawyer Barry Scheck. "Definitely. By far," replied Gerdes. His two-day testimony inventoried police methods that, he said, "created unacceptable risks" of cross-contamination, from using outdated chemicals to placing test tubes side-by-side to wearing the same gloves for more than one test.

Cross-examining, Deputy District Attorney George Clarke got Gerdes to admit he had never examined another laboratory so scrupulously. Clarke also brought out Gerdes's long-standing opposition to DNA testing based on the PCR (polymerase chain reaction) process, yet got him to concede that RFLP (restriction fragment length polymorphism) testing was reliable.

DETECTIVE FUHRMAN A RACIST

In North Carolina, on August 7, the Court of Appeals ruled that the tape recordings and testimony of Laura Hart McKinny, the screenwriter and professor whom Mark Fuhrman served as an adviser, "could reasonably make a difference in the outcome of the trial." This meant that Judge Ito could rule on whether the jury could hear the tapes.

The defense called Dr. Michael Baden, a forensic pathologist, who contradicted the earlier testimony of Dr. Lakshmanan Sathyavagiswaran. Both victims fought hard, he said, and could have struggled for as long as 15 minutes and could have left marks on the killer. Cross-examining, Deputy District Attorney Kelberg depicted the witness as a publicity-seeking hired gun whose services to the defense had already earned him more than $100,000.

The transcript for the O.J. Simpson trial numbered 50,000 pages.

Meantime, at the defense table, Simpson and his lawyers were reading the transcripts of the taped conversations between detective Mark Fuhrman and Laura Hart McKinny as well as her screenplay draft based on the conversations.

Next day, defense attorney Cochran told the press that the transcripts disclosed that detective Fuhrman used the word "nigger" at least 30 times in the taped interviews and that, at least 17 times, he referred to lying and covering up for fellow officers or to planting evidence. In addition, Fuhrman slandered Jews, blacks, and women, including Judge Ito's wife, police captain Margaret York, for whom the detective had once worked. "I am the most important witness in the trial of the century," said Fuhrman on one tape. "If I go down, their case goes bye bye."

"And that's what they're faced with—bye bye," Cochran told the press. "This is a blockbuster. This is a bombshell. This is perhaps the biggest thing that has happened in any case in this country in this decade, and they know it."

Judge Ito faced the possibility that his wife, the highest-ranking woman in the LAPD, might be called to rebut Fuhrman's racist remarks. Prosecutor Clark demanded that the judge withdraw from the case since California law prevents judges from presiding in cases in which they or their spouses have "personal knowledge of disputed evidentiary facts." The tapes, she said, were "the cornerstone" of the defense's "very cynical and crude effort to pull this jury away from the evidence." If the tapes were admitted, she added, she would call Captain York to testify that she barely remembered Fuhrman. This would cast doubt on whether the officer knew the captain long enough to ridicule her.

A breathless courtroom listened as the judge, almost in tears, said, "I love my wife dearly. I am wounded by criticism of her, as any spouse would be. The appearance of a reasonable concern that this court could not impartially rule is there." Therefore, he said, he would step aside temporarily while another judge decided whether the tapes were admissible.

Twenty-four hours later, Marcia Clark retracted her demand that Judge Ito withdraw.

While justice was slow for O.J. Simpson on the West Coast, it moved swiftly for Susan Smith on the East Coast: Smith confessed to drowning her two children in a lake outside Union, South Carolina—but only after claiming the boys had been abducted by a car-jacker, a black man she described to authorities. A South Carolina Court ruled Smith could not plead guilty by reasons of insanity and moved toward determining her sentence. Thirteen days after seating the jury, the sentence of life in prison was handed down, sparing Smith the death sentence the prosecution had sought.

The sequestered jury heard none of the controversy over the Fuhrman tapes, and on Friday, August 18, Los Angeles County Superior Court Judge John H. Reid ruled that there was "no reasonable expectation" that Captain York would be a relevant witness.

Dr. Henry C. Lee, head of the Connecticut State Police Crime Laboratory, took the stand. First, with red ink, an eyedropper, cotton bond paper, and the palm of his hand, he educated the jury on how blood might drip, spatter, or flick, or be smeared, rubbed, or banged, to create such evidence as "impact spatters," "satellite spatters," and "angular deposits." It was a demonstration with which the affable Chinese native had long since earned widespread admiration among American trial lawyers. Defense attorney Barry L. Scheck focused Dr. Lee's testimony on faint parallel lines found on the walkway at Bundy as well as on an envelope and piece of paper found near the victims. Were the marks from a shoe? One *could* be from a shoe, said Lee, but not from the Italian-made Bruno Magli shoes established by the prosecution as the source of shoe prints at the crime scene. Deputy District Attorney Hank Goldberg's plodding cross-examination tried to dispel the possibilities hinted at by Dr. Lee's testimony: that more than one assailant might have committed the murders, and that tampering might have changed blood samples collected at Bundy.

Tuesday, August 29, the jury began a long hiatus from the courtroom. That morning, Judge Ito shared with all the world— except the 14 panelists—the apparent certainty that Mark Fuhrman was a perjurer, a racist, and a "rogue" policeman who practiced arresting citizens without probable cause, destroying exculpatory evidence, inventing accusations, disregarding legal precedent, pounding confessions from those accused, and adapting testimony to his whim. Laura Hart McKinny told the packed courtroom—with extra lawyers for both sides seated in the jury box—how she had audiotaped 16 hours of interviews with Fuhrman as journalistic resource material.

Defense attorney Gerald Uelmen argued that the judge should let the jury hear all 41 times that Fuhrman, who had testified under oath that he had not used the word "nigger" in the last 10 years, had in fact voiced that word. Prosecutor Clark countered. The real "N word," she said, is not "nigger" but "Nicole." "None of this is relevant," she said. "The admission of this evidence is telling the jury: 'Disregard the case. Look somewhere else.'"

Next day, the judge ruled that only two of Fuhrman's 41 references to blacks as "niggers" could be played for the jury. He also said the defense had failed to provide sufficient evidence of the suggested misconduct—the moving of the bloody glove from Bundy to Rockingham—of which it accused Fuhrman.

The defense team was outraged. Cochran asked the judge to reconsider. "You could walk down the street a block and a half to the Court of Appeals," said the judge, "if you don't like the ruling."

Tuesday, September 5, the day after Labor Day, brought the jury back. It heard Kathleen Bell, Natalie Singer, and Laura Hart McKinny each testify to hearing Fuhrman use the racial epithet within the past 10 years.

On Wednesday morning, Deputy District Attorney Christopher Darden cross-examined Hart McKinny, suggesting she was trying to sell her tapes to *Inside Edition* and *The National Inquirer* through her lawyers. "What is *Inside Edition*?" she responded.

The defense next introduced Roderic Hodge, a black man who related how Fuhrman, when arresting him in 1987, said, "I told you we'd get you, nigger." With that, Simpson's lawyers said they were almost ready to rest their case.

The jury was again sent away. Mark Fuhrman, still under oath from his March appearance, took the stand, his lawyer beside him. Defense attorney Uelmen asked: "Was the testimony that you gave in the preliminary hearing in this case completely truthful?" "Have you ever falsified a police report?" "Did you plant or manufacture any evidence in this case?"

To each question, Fuhrman replied, "I wish to assert my Fifth Amendment privilege."

Uelmen asked if he intended to give the same reply to any question asked. "Yes," said Fuhrman. The judge dismissed him.

Might Fuhrman be called, with the jury present, to be asked questions sure to make him invoke the Fifth Amendment? No, ruled Ito. He cited several California cases that held that, because a jury was apt to perceive an admission of guilt, a witness could not be forced to take the Fifth. But the judge announced that he would instruct the jury: "Detective Mark Fuhrman is not available for further testimony as a witness in this case. His unavailability for further testimony on cross-examination is a factor which you may consider in evaluating his credibility as a witness."

Prosecutor Clark objected emphatically. The judge said she could file an appeal. She did so, and, within three hours, justices Paul Turner and Orville J. Armstrong of the California Court of Appeals ruled that "the proposed instruction regarding the unavailability of Detective Fuhrman is not to be given."

REBUTTALS GET UNDER WAY

By Tuesday, September 12, the courtroom was seething with impatience and anger fueled by exhaustion and frustration. O.J. Simpson had spent 453 days in jail, the jury had been sequestered for 245 days, the prosecution had presented 58 witnesses, and the defense had introduced 53.

The defense asked the judge either to strike the Fuhrman testimony about finding the glove behind the Rockingham house or to return the detective to the stand. The judge refused. Defense counsel Cochran filed an appeal and refused to rest his case until the appeal decision came down. Ito then ordered the prosecution to start its rebuttal case before the defense had closed.

Again the judge rejected a prosecution request to let jurors know that fibers on the Rockingham glove were an extremely rare type found only in a few Broncos (the prosecution, he ruled, had failed to give the evidence to the defense in time).

The defense lost its appeal as the California Court of Appeals ruled that jurors could not be informed of Fuhrman's Fifth Amendment plea. Nor might the jury draw adverse conclusions from his absence. The defense appealed to a higher court.

Next, the prosecution brought back glove expert Richard Rubin and showed videotapes of Simpson wearing gloves during football broadcasts—the same gloves, testified Rubin, as the bloody pair in evidence.

Prosecution witness Gary Sims, of the California Department of Justice, testified that new DNA testing proved that blood on the Bronco's center console was both Goldman's and Simpson's. FBI agent Douglas Deedrick challenged defense witness Dr. Lee's testimony that lines on Goldman's jeans and on paper found near the bodies might have come from shoe prints of a second murderer. Rather, they matched the ribbed texture of Goldman's shirt. FBI footprint expert William Bodziak pointed out that the lines matched no shoe print he had ever seen. He added that what Dr. Lee had characterized as "imprints" on the Bundy walkway were impressions made in the concrete when it was poured.

As the defense rebuttal of the prosecution rebuttal began, Judge Ito banished all photographers, sketch artists, and TV from the courtroom while Larry and Craig Fiato, brothers from organized crime who were under FBI protection, testified. They said that detective Vannatter told them, in casual conversations over beer and cigarettes, that the police had gone to Rockingham not to notify Simpson of the deaths—as Vannatter had earlier testified—but because he was a suspect. The brothers' testimony, said the defense, combined with the police search of Rockingham without a warrant, proved that the police had pushed a "rush to judgment."

Countering, the prosecution called West Los Angeles police commander Keith Bushey to review his orders to notify Simpson as quickly as possible. Defense attorney Cochran berated Bushey for notifying Simpson as—because of divorce—he was not next of kin.

On September 21, the California Supreme Court rejected the defense appeal to reinstate Judge Ito's forbidden instruction to the jury about Fuhrman. Meantime, Ito ruled the jury would not be limited to an all-or-nothing verdict. He agreed with the prosecution that their version of the murders—in which the defendant was accused of planning and premeditation by wearing gloves and dark clothing and carrying a sharp knife—constituted first-degree murder. But, he ruled, the verdict might be second-degree murder if the jury concluded that Simpson acted in a fit of passion or uncontrollable rage.

On September 22, Cochran said the defense rested its case, then (as expected in any trial) moved for acquittal (motion denied), then quietly said his client "would like to make a brief statement." Prosecutor Clark objected vehemently: "This is a very obvious defense bid to get material admitted through conjugal visits that is not admitted in court. Please don't do this, your Honor. I beg you."

Simpson stood up. "I am mindful of the mood and the stamina of this jury," he said. "I have confidence of their integrity... that they will find... that I did not, could not, and would not have committed this crime... I have four kids—two kids I haven't seen in a year. They ask me every week, 'Dad, how much longer...?'"

"All right," the judge cut in. Then he asked Simpson if he understood that he had a right to testify. "Yes," said Simpson.

Both sides rested. Later, a defense lawyer revealed that Simpson, coached by Cochran and attorney Robert Kardashian, had rehearsed his statement for two weeks.

CLOSING ARGUMENTS

Summations began on September 26—one year after jury selection began. Prosecutor Clark urged the jury to "weed out the smoke and mirrors and sideshow" and avoid the "false roads" mapped out by the defense. She took the Fuhrman bull by the horns: "Is he a racist? Yes. Is he the worst LAPD has to offer? Yes. Should LAPD ever have hired him? No. In fact, do we wish there were no such person on the planet? Yes. But . . . it would be a tragedy if you found the defendant not guilty because of the racist attitude of one police officer."

Moment by moment, Clark tracked, on a large display board, the whereabouts of the defendant on the night of the murders. Between 9:36 and 10:54, she pointed to a gap marked "Defendant's Whereabouts Unknown." Next, she detailed the timing of the thumps on Kato's wall, the silliness of defense contentions that blood was planted and DNA was "flying all over the place," the match that made Simpson "one in 57 billion people that could have left that blood," and the trail of blood down the Bundy walkway, into the Bronco, and into the Rockingham house.

Prosecutor Darden reviewed Nicole Brown Simpson's last months, her ex-husband's attempts to control her, the burning fuse—destined sooner or later to produce an explosion of rage—of their relationship.

Defense counsel Cochran summed up. Building an analogy between all the evidence and the defendant's futile attempt to put on the glove before the jury, he repeatedly said, "If it doesn't fit, you must acquit." He suggested that professional killers, who might have been targeting Ron Goldman, were the actual murderers. He quoted Cicero, Lincoln, and Frederick Douglass. He lambasted the police work and "untrained officers" who "traipsed through the evidence." He said the 911 call prompted by Simpson's breaking down a door was "an unfortunate incident between two people who were married," and "there was no physical violence." As to the "whereabouts unknown" time line, he repeatedly reminded the jury that the defendant "doesn't have to prove anything." He mounted displays to itemize "Fuhrman's Big Lies" and "Vannatter's Big Lies." Finally, he compared Fuhrman's racist attitude to that of Hitler and advised the jurors that in acquitting Simpson they would become custodians of the Constitution and saviors of the Los Angeles Police Department.

The "contaminated, corrupted, and compromised" physical evidence, said defense attorney Scheck in reviewing the defense's contention that evidence was planted, was "a cancer infecting the heart of this case." Then Cochran challenged the prosecution to answer 15 questions as it closed its final statement.

The prosecution ignored his questions. Prosecutor Darden reminded the jury—in his slow, deliberate delivery that contrasted with the passionate style of defense counsel Cochran—that "no one's above the law . . . Simpson isn't above the law."

"I looked in the Constitution," Darden told the three-quarters black jury that Cochran had admonished to take custody of that document, "and you know what I saw? The Constitution said that Ron and Nicole had the right to liberty, the right to life, the right to the pursuit of happiness. And I looked to see if it said anything about O.J. Simpson. And it said that a man has no right to kill and then get away with it because one of the investigating officers is a racist."

Completing the summation, Marcia Clark reviewed the principal evidence point by point despite a constant barrage of objections by defense attorneys Cochran and Scheck. On a final display board, she cited one item of evidence after another that was "uncontradicted" and "unrefuted." Then she played once more the frantic 911 calls of Nicole Brown Simpson: "He's back. He's O.J. Simpson. I think you know his record."

"Ron and Nicole, they're speaking to you," concluded prosecutor Clark. "They are both telling you who did it, with their hair, their clothes, their bodies, their blood. They tell you he did it. They told you in the only way they can. Will you hear them? Or will you ignore their plea for justice?"

It was Friday afternoon, September 29. Judge Ito briefly charged the jury. They retired to elect their foreman.

Deliberations began at 10:00 A.M. on Monday. Shortly, the jury filed in to hear the testimony of limousine driver Allan Park read back to them. Then, less than four hours after beginning their discussion, they announced they had reached a verdict. The foreman handed Judge Ito a sealed envelope. He said it would be opened the next morning at 10:00 Pacific time.

THE VERDICT

On Tuesday, October 3, people across the country gathered in front of televisions and radios to await the announcement of the jury's decision in this "trial of the century": The jury found Orenthal James Simpson not guilty of all charges.

While many rejoiced at the announcement, others remained disappointed that ultimately the trial had not been about murder but about race. Meanwhile, O.J. Simpson returned to his Rockingham home in a fashion that was eerily similar to the now-famous freeway chase of the white Ford Bronco: Two white vans, one of them carrying the acquitted Simpson, were followed by media helicopters as they made their way through the streets of Los Angeles where on-lookers held signs and cheered.

In the days following the verdict, the 12 jurors and two alternates returned to the business of everyday living, legal analysts continued to discuss the case, and TV talk show hosts interviewed the victims' families as well as "Dream Team" lawyers (among whom a rift had developed). While O.J. Simpson promised to find Nicole's and Mr. Goldman's killer(s), the Los Angeles Police and District Attorney made statements that the investigation into the murders was closed.

—Bernard Ryan, Jr.

GLOSSARY

Note: References to other defined terms are set in bold type.

Accessory after the fact: one who obstructs justice by giving comfort or assistance to the felon (*see* **felony**), knowing that the felon has committed a crime or is sought by authorities in connection with a serious crime

Accessory before the fact: one who aids in the commission of a **felony** by ordering or encouraging it, but who is not present when the crime is perpetrated

Accomplice: one who voluntarily engages with another in the commission or attempted commission of a crime

Arraignment: the procedure by which a criminal defendant is brought before the trial court and informed of the charges against him or her and the pleas (guilty, not guilty, or no contest) he or she may enter in response

Change of venue: the removal of a lawsuit from a county or district to another for trial, often permitted in criminal cases where the court finds that the defendant would not receive a fair trial in the first location because of adverse publicity

Circumstantial evidence: indirect, secondary facts from which the existence or non-existence of a fact at issue in a case may be inferred

Co-conspirator: one who engages in a **conspiracy** with others; the acts and declarations of any one conspirator are admissible as evidence against all his or her co-conspirators

Common law: principles and rules of action derived from past judicial decisions, as distinct from laws created solely through legislative enactment

Compensatory damages: monetary damages the law awards to compensate an injured party solely for the injured sustained because of the action of another (*see also* **Punitive damages**)

Conspiracy: the agreement of two or more individuals to commit, through their joint efforts, an unlawful act

Coroner's inquest: an examination by the coroner, often with the aid of a jury, into the causes of a death occurring under suspicious circumstances

Cross-examination: questioning a witness, by a party or a lawyer other than the one who is called the witness, about testimony the witness gave on **direct examination**

Direct evidence: testimony at trial by a witness who actually heard the words or saw the actions that, if believed by the trier of fact, conclusively establish a fact at issue

Direct examination: initial questioning of a witness by the lawyer who called him or her, the purpose of which is to present testimony regarding the facts of the examining party's case

Double Jeopardy: a bar against double prosecution or double punishment for the same offense, operational only in criminal cases and only if there is no appeal of a conviction

Due process applicable only to actions of state or federal governments and their officials, it guarantees fairness when the state deprives an individual of property or liberty; also, substantive due process requires that all legislation be enacted solely to further legitimate governmental objectives

Extradition: the surrender by one state or country of an individual who is accused or convicted of an offense outside the borders of that state or country

Expert witness: a witness, such as a psychological statistician or ballistics expert, with special knowledge concerning the subject he or she will testify about

Felony: high crimes, such as burglary, rape, or homicide, which unlike misdemeanors, are often punishable by lengthy jail terms or death

Gag order: a court order restricting dissemination, by attorneys and witnesses, of information about a case (such orders directed at the press are unconstitutional); also, an order to restrain an unruly defendant who is disrupting his or her trial

Grand jury: traditionally consisting of twenty-three (as opposed to twelve- or six-member **petit juries**) individuals empaneled to determine whether the facts and accusations presented by prosecutors in criminal proceedings warrant an **indictment** and trial of the accused

Habeas corpus: a procedure for a judicial ruling on the legality of an individual's custody, used in a criminal context to challenge a convict's confinement and in a civil context to challenge child custody, deportation, and commitment to a mental institution

Hearsay: a statement, other than one made by a witness at a hearing or trial, offered to prove the truth of a matter asserted at the hearing or trial; such statements are inadmissable as evidence except under certain circumstances

Immunity: exemption from a duty or penalty; witnesses are often granted immunity from prosecution in order to compel them to respond questions they might otherwise refuse to answer based on the Fifth Amendment's privilege against self- incrimination

Impeach: to call into question the truthfulness of a witness's testimony by offering evidence of his or her lack of veracity

Indictment: a formal written accusation drawn up by a public prosecuting attorney and issued by a grand jury against a party charged with a crime

Injunction: a judicial remedy requiring a party to cease or refrain from some specified action

In re: literally, "in the matter of"; used to signify a legal proceeding where there are no adversaries, but merely a matter, such as an estate, requiring judicial action

Judicial review: review of a trial court decision by an appellate court; power and responsibility of the U.S. Supreme Court and the highest state courts to determine the constitutionality of the acts of the legislatures and executive branches of their respective jurisdictions

Jury tampering: a criminal offense consisting of attempting to improperly influence one or more jurors' vote(s) by threats, bribes, etc.

Justifiable homicide: the killing of another in self-defense or in the lawful defense of one's property; killing another when the law demands it, such as in execution for a capital crime

Manslaughter: unlawful killing of another without malice, aforethought, or an intent to cause death, it calls for less severe penalties than murder; most jurisdictions distinguish between voluntary, or intentional manslaughter, and involuntary manslaughter, such as a death resulting from an automobile accident

Misdemeanor: any criminal offense less serious than a **felony**, generally punishable by a fine or imprisonment other than in a penitentiary and for a shorter period than would be imposed for a **felony**

Mistrial: a trial declared void before a verdict is returned, usually because the jury is deadlocked or because some incurable and fundamental error that is prejudicial to the defendant

Original jurisdiction: the authority to hear a case at its inception and to pass judgment on its law and facts, as opposed to **appellate jurisdiction**, which grants the power to review the decisions of lower tribunals, which can then be affirmed, reversed, or modified

Parole: a conditional release of a prisoner after he or she has served part of a sentence

Perjury: the criminal offense of making false statements while under oath

Petit jury: an ordinary trial jury, as opposed to a **grand jury**, traditionally composed of twelve (in some jurisdictions six) persons whose job it is to determine issues of fact in civil and criminal proceedings

Plaintiff: the party who initiates a lawsuit, seeking a remedy for an injury to his or her rights

Prima facie case: a case that, because it is supported by the requisite minimum of evidence and is free of obvious defects, can go to the jury; thus the defendant is required to proceed with its case rather than move for dismissal or a directed verdict

Punitive damages: compensation in excess of actual losses awarded to a successful

Plaintiff: who was injured under circumstances involving malicious and willful misconduct on the part of the defendant (*see also***Compensatory damages**)

Reasonable doubt: the degree of certainty required for a juror to find a criminal defendant guilty, meaning that proof of guilt must be so clear that an ordinary person would have no reasonable doubt as to the guilt of the defendant

RICO laws: "Racketeer Influenced and Corrupt Organization Act," federal statute designed to prosecute organized crime; many states have enacted similar statutes

Statutory rape: the crime of having sexual intercourse with a female under an age set by the state statute

Subpoena: a written order issued under court authority compelling the appearance of a witness at a judicial proceeding

Temporary insanity: a criminal defense asserting that, because the accused was legally insane at the time the crime was committed, he or she did not have the necessary mental state to commit it and is therefore not responsible for the alleged criminal conduct

Voir dire: examination by the court or by lawyers for the parties of prospective jurors; also, a hearing by the court during the trial out of the jury's presence to determine initially a question of law

Writ of *habeas corpus*: a procedure used in criminal contexts to bring a petitioning prisoner before the court to determine the legality of his or her confinement (*see **habeas corpus***)

INDEX

INDEX